REVISED EDITION

Put to the Test

An Educator's and Consumer's Guide to Standardized Testing

by Gerald W. Bracey

The Omnipresence of Tests and Why You Need to Know About Them

D1502081

WRITTEN BY
Gerald W. Bracey

EDITED BY
Bruce Smith

DESIGNED BY
Joyce Koeper
Peg Caudell
Debbie Webb

ILLUSTRATIONS BY
Jem Sullivan

PUBLISHED BY
Center for Professional Development & Services

Phi Delta Kappa International
408 N. Union Street
Bloomington, Indiana
47402-0789
812/339-1156

Revised Edition 2002

Introduction to the Revised Edition

I was tempted to title this revised edition *The Tyranny of Testing*. Unfortunately, Banesh Hoffman used this title back in 1962 although the tyranny he had in mind was that of the multiple-choice item.

I have spent a fair amount of time over the last 25 years being astonished by the growing role of testing in American education. Just when I would think, "things cannot get any crazier," they always have. Testing was once a tool. Now it's a juggernaut, a weapon to be used for political and social control.

If it gets worse, we might end up like the Koreans where high school students' futures are determined by their scores on a single national test. Many South Korean mothers spend a couple of hours each day in temple praying for their children's success on the test for 99 days. On 100th day, the eve of the national examination, they pray all night. Hands up; clasp hands in prayer; bow; down on knees; head to floor; back on haunches clasp hands in prayer. Repeat 3,000 times.

On exam day, Korean workers report an hour late. They don't want to clog the streets and risk making the students late. On arrival at the test sites, the students are greeted by shouting crowds waving banners. Even the United States gets into the act: all 90 American military bases stop training for nine hours on exam day.

The mothers want their kids to get into one of the three top-ranked universities in Korea. These universities will get 873,000 applications and accept 15,000 — 1.7%. Those 15,000, the lucky few, are headed for the good jobs.

I didn't make this up. All of it appeared in the November 16, 2000 edition of Singapore's *Straits Times*. I don't think we'll ever go to this extreme, but we're headed in that direction. Just read the 10 scenes from the world of testing that appear in Chapter 2.

We've gone test mad.

As an exercise in perspective-building, I suggest you read and think about the following qualities that tests *don't* measure:

Creativity	Civic mindedness
Critical thinking	Self-awareness
Resilience	Self-discipline
Motivation	Empathy
Persistence	Leadership
Humor	Compassion
Reliability	Curiosity
Enthusiasm	

After the events of September 11, 2001, I added two more:

Courage	Cowardice

If you consider this list seriously, it is easy to see how test-obsessed we have become. It is appropriate, and relatively easy, to formulate arguments against testing — at least against certain kinds of testing. That is not what this book is about. For those arguments, I refer you to *The Case Against Standardized Testing*, by Alfie Kohn; *Standardized Minds*, by Peter Sacks; and *One Size Fits Few* and *Caught in the Middle*, by Susan Ohanian. (These books, and others of different perspectives, are provided in the "Resources" section of this book on page 95.)

Most of this book is devoted to informing you about what tests are and aren't. Not that there will be any doubt about my opinions of some of the things that are. But I encounter many people who reject tests without really knowing what they are rejecting. This puts them at a decided disadvantage in arguments about tests. A state that develops tests, like Virginia, also appoints psychometricians — professionals in the field of testing — as an advisory board. These people know the ins and outs of testing and add credibility to the state's efforts, no matter how shamefully the state might be acting.

But hiring psychometricians to advise you on testing is like hiring the Pope and a few cardinals to advise you on birth control. The psychometricians will advise on issues of reliability or validity. They won't question the ethics of the testing program.

To be an informed consumer, you need to be comfortable with tests and the terminology surrounding tests. Thomas Kane and Douglas Staiger, two non-psychometricians at Stanford University's Hoover Institution and Dartmouth University, respectively, made this telling comment in a paper: "Most of these [school accountability] programs have been set up with very little recognition of the strengths and weaknesses of the measures they're based on."[1] The reason that the people who set the testing programs up don't recognize the strengths and weaknesses is because those people don't *care* about strengths and weaknesses. They have a political or an ideological agenda or both.

Testing in America today is about power, control, and ideology. It is not about education.

Politicians who get tough on schools through testing or who often say "schools must be accountable" mostly don't have a clue as to what they mean by accountability or what a fair system would look like. They often offer simplistic answers to complicated problems. As long as test scores rise, they're happy. This can lead to programs that make no sense. For instance, North Carolina and Texas have been singled out recently for test score gains. Yet, in the original version of the Bush "No Child Left Behind" legislation, some 97% of these two states' schools would have been labeled failures.

You shouldn't be clueless about testing. That's dangerous.

Indeed, a group of testing professionals recently expressed doubts that the public knew about the range of negative consequences from high-stakes testing: "Moreover, it seems certain that few people are aware of limits on the information that tests can provide. No survey questions, for example, have asked how much measurement error is acceptable when used to make high-stakes decisions about individual students. The support for testing expressed in polls might decline if the public understood these things."[2]

If you don't know the difference between a percentile rank and a normal-curve equivalent — two common way of reporting test scores — you're at a disadvantage. You're at a disadvantage arguing with someone who does know the difference, of course, but you're also at a disadvantage arguing with people who *don't* because you can't tell that they don't know.

The rest of this book deals largely with the world as it *is*, not the world as I would like it to be. I think the situations reported from the testing scene are dreadful. But they represent the world that is.

One of the opening lines of the first chapter of this book is "People might judge your competence as a teacher on the basis of tests." I think that's awful, but it is what is. If you want to know if the judgments are reasonable, you need to know something about tests. Emotional arguments won't cut it. I think we have lost our concept of childhood as a special time, and I think that tests have played a large role in that loss. We treat kids these days as miniature adults. Arguments based on the "special time" of childhood won't cut it. You need to frame the argument in the terms the testers use.

I hope this book will help you do that.

No book about testing can be thin and complete. This book does not deal with two hot sets of issues concerning testing: special education and bilingual education. Those deserve their own separate treatments, but they are beyond the scope of this book.

Gerald W. Bracey
February 2002

TABLE OF CONTENTS

CHAPTER 1

Why You Should Read This Book

There are a variety of reasons why people should read this book depending on just who they are and what their connection is to the schools.

Teachers: People might judge your competence as a teacher on the basis of tests. You might get a raise, a promotion, or a termination notice based on how your students perform.

Administrators: Your job might ride on test scores. Your district might lose its accreditation based on test scores. Your school's or district's funding might depend in part on test scores. The state might take over your district based on test scores. You need to be able to expand upon the "box score" reporting used by so many newspapers.

Parents: Your children might or might not graduate from high school depending on how well they perform on tests. They might or might not be promoted to the next grade based on their test scores. They might or might not get into programs for the gifted and talented or be given special education services because of their test scores. They might or might not get into the college or graduate school of their choice if their test scores are judged to be too low. Your children's academic performance will almost certainly be reported to you in the form of test scores. Will you be able to understand and use them? Will you know when you should question or yell at school authorities?

Students: All of the reasons that apply to parents apply to you as well. Test scores might also help or

hinder your decision about which colleges to apply to. Should they? They will almost certainly play some role in determining whether or not you get into college; at selective colleges, the role could be a significant one. They might determine, to a large extent, whether or not you get a fellowship to that college. If you want to go on to graduate school, test scores will play a role.

Citizens: Members of all of the above groups and citizens-at-large might well find the schools in their state judged on the basis of test scores. At the 1996 "Education Summit," the nation's governors expressed great interest in establishing standards and in creating assessments by which to evaluate the performance of their schools on the standards and by which to compare their states one to another. Even whole nations are rated and ranked on the basis of how well their 9- and 13-year-old students bubble in answer sheets. Are these rankings fair? Important? In 2000, many stories in the Michigan media bragged about that state's performance in an international comparison. Were they blowing smoke?

President Clinton kept stating that he wanted his legacy to be in the area of education. How did he propose to establish this legacy? In large part, by establishing national tests in reading and mathematics. President Bush was elected in November 2000 and by January 2001 he had sent to Congress an education proposal. Its central feature? A testing program. Bush wanted to test all students in grades 3 through 8, every year, in reading, mathematics, science, and social studies.

On October 3, 2001, the executive directors of many professional education organizations met to decide whether they would or would not support Bush's bill. Subsequently, the National Conference of State Legislatures came out in opposition. Of the professional associations, only the American Association of School Administrators opposed the legislation; the rest simply said they could not support it. Many hoped that the conference committee, convened to reconcile the House and Senate versions of the bill, would give up, go home, and start from scratch. But they were wrong. The conference committee reached agreement in December 2001.

One of the aspects of Bush's proposal is the concept of "Adequate Yearly Progress." Schools must show it, although no one has yet figured out how (partly because it's a nutty idea). Most of the evidence for or against a school will come from test scores. As Thomas Toch wrote in the November 2001 issue of the Washington Monthly, Bush's plan "hurts the nation's students more than it helps them; promotes lower rather than higher standards; misleads the public about school performance; pushes top teachers out of schools where they are most needed; and drives down the level of instruction in many classrooms." That's quite an accomplishment for an "Education President."

The final version of the Bush program leaves it to each state to set standards and to define Adequate Yearly Progress. However, such definition must be statistically reliable and valid. This is an interesting requirement since no one has yet figured out how to define the concept. No matter how it is defined or measured, though, all students in a state must attain a "proficient" level within 12 years. This timeline ensures two things: 1) most of those who created the legislation won't be around when its full impact is felt, and 2) states will, as Toch has predicted, adopt low standards in order to be able to demonstrate progress.

Schools that do not show Adequate Yearly Progress for two consecutive years are subject to an escalating set of responses. First, they get some money and technical assistance from the state (though no states are currently set up to provide such assistance). If test scores do not improve, teachers and administrators can be transferred, the school can be restructured, or the entire district can be abolished. During all of these proceedings, all pupils at the problem schools have the option of choosing to attend another, higher performing school in the same district. How they will find seats there is not specified, but the districts are responsible for providing transportation. Thus at a time when states are cutting hundreds of millions of dollars from their budgets because of declining revenues, the Bush Administration and Congress have burdened them with huge, test-based, unfunded mandates.

It is clear that tests are important to us in our daily lives. Unfortunately, there is a great deal more you should know about the uses and abuses of testing in America. Myths and misconceptions abound surrounding the ways in which tests are made and used. It is not the case that a test is a test is a test. Tests are like automobiles: sedans, vans, and sports

TerraNova CTBS Complete Battery

Comprehensive Tests of Basic Skills

STUDENTS	SCORES	Read	Vocab	Read Cmpst	Lang	Lang Mech	Lang Cmpst	Math	Math Cmpst	Math Total	Total Score**	Spell	WORD ANLYS
Student #1	NP	65	44	55	61	73	68	67	48	61	61	50	71
DOB: 5/4/91	NS	6	5	5	6	6	6	6	5	6	6	5	6
Age: 8 yr 11 mo	GE	4.7	3.6	4.1	4.5	5.1	4.8	4.5	3.7	4.1	4.3	3.8	N/A
Form: A Level: 13	NCE	58	47	53	56	63	60	60	49	56	56	50	62
	AANCE	67	65	66	64	64	65	64	56	62	66	64	63
Student #2	NP	96	89	95	91	*99	98	98	92	97	97	93	97
DOB: 9/25/90	NS	9	7	8	8	9	9	9	8	9	9	8	9
Age: 9 yr 7 mo	GE	11.6	7.8	10.2	10.1	12.+	11.5	8.2	5.3	6.5	9.9	7.5	N/A
Form: A Level: 13	NCE	88	76	85	78	99	93	93	79	90	89	81	91
	AANCE	65	62	64	62	64	65	66	62	67	66	57	63
Student #3	NP	66	43	55	75	*99	95	91	*99	98	91	99	97
DOB: 8/10/91	NS	6	5	5	6	9	8	8	9	9	8	9	9
Age: 8 yr 8 mo	GE	4.8	3.6	4.1	5.7	12.+	10.2	6.4	8.1	7.4	7.7	10.7	N/A
Form: A Level: 13	NCE	58	46	53	64	99	86	78	99	95	78	99	91
	AANCE	60	59	60	59	60	60	60	54	59	61	57	58

TEST OF COGNITIVE SKILLS SECOND EDITION

Scores	NON VRB	MEM	VRB	TOT
NPA	76	75	88	86
NPA	95	*86	66	92
NPA	94	54	74	88

NORMS FROM: 1996
TEST DATE: 4/3/00
SCORING: PATTERN (IRT)
QUARTER MONTH: 31
CITY: SCHOOL:
STATE: DISTRICT:

NP: National Percentile
NS: National Stanine
GE: Grade Equivalent
NCE: Normal Curve Equivalent
AANCE: Anticipated Normal Curve Equivalent

NPA: National Percentile by Age

*:   Maximum or Minimum Score

**:   Total Score consists of Reading Composite, Language Composite, and Math Composite

Adapted version of Class Record Sheet reproduced with written permission of the McGraw-Hill Companies, Inc.

cars differ from one another in important ways, and so do different kinds of tests. To use tests wisely we need to know something about them. Otherwise, we get used by them.

Parents, teachers, students, administrators: Take a look at the report above. This is an actual report from which students' names have been removed to protect their privacy. Does this sheet make sense to you?

The first student has "NPs" that vary from 44 to 73. Is this 29 percentile rank difference across different subject areas common to most students? The second student has all percentile ranks above 90. His score on "language mechanics" has a grade equivalent of 12+, meaning that the score is higher than that attained by a high school senior. How can this be possible? The third student has a range of

scores from the 43rd percentile to the 99th. This is a huge range. What's going on here? In addition, none of this student's high scores are predicted to be so high. What's happening?

Why does the report show five different scores? What do they all mean? Why are the differences between NP and NCE sometimes large and sometimes small? Why are the differences between NCE and AANCE sometimes large and sometimes small? What do the scores on the right side of the page mean? How do they relate to the scores on the left side of the page?

This book is for people with any difficulty or lack of confidence in answering these questions. All of them are addressed in Appendix 1 at the end of the book.

TEST YOUR KNOWLEDGE OF TESTING

We begin this booklet with a pop quiz. The answers and a short explanation for each question appear on the next page. A more complete explanation can be found in the chapters that follow. The questions are all true-false. Good luck.

1. (T) (F) If a school district's high school graduates do not all read at grade level, the district is not doing its job of educating the students.

2. (T) (F) If the average total SAT score at the university you most want to go to is 1100 and your total SAT score is only 1040, you shouldn't bother to apply.

3. (T) (F) If in the Mark Twain School, Mrs. Smith's students do not score as high as Mrs. Jones' students, Mrs. Smith is not as good a teacher as Mrs. Jones.

4. (T) (F) If a school adopts a new curriculum and test scores fall, the new curriculum is shown to be inferior to the old curriculum.

5. (T) (F) The scores on a test naturally fall along a "normal"— bell-shaped — curve.

6. (T) (F) If two curricula are compared and the students using curriculum A score statistically significantly higher than the students using curriculum B, then curriculum A is the better curriculum.

7. (T) (F) A fourth-grade student reading at seventh-grade level should be promoted to the seventh grade, at least for reading instruction.

8. (T) (F) The SAT is a "common yardstick," meaning that two students with the same score from different states have the same potential for college.

9. (T) (F) If a child who scored at the 63rd percentile in reading one year falls to the 57th percentile in the next year, something is wrong. Either the child isn't trying, or the second year's teacher is not as effective.

10. (T) (F) Research indicates that IQ is 80% inherited.

THE ANSWERS

All of the statements on the preceding page are false. Here are the brief explanations of why.

1. Most tests define "grade level" as the score of the average child at a given grade. For a particular school, all children could possibly be above grade level — if the school were excellent or located in an affluent neighborhood or both. But nationally, half of all students are, by definition, below average — that is, below grade level.

2. If the average total SAT score is 1100, this means that half the incoming freshmen are accepted with scores below this average.[3] Your 1040 might well be acceptable. In addition, you are not in competition with all other applicants. If that were true, universities would not only be unable to field athletic teams, but they would also be unable to have fine arts or performing arts departments. Like athletes, students with these special talents often have trouble with paper-and-pencil tests. However, if your daddy went to the same school or can afford to pay all of your expenses, your chances of admission are mightily improved.

3. There are many possible reasons why the classes could differ. Mrs. Smith might not emphasize material that the test covers as much as Mrs. Jones does. Mrs. Smith might also be a newer teacher; veteran teachers are often rewarded by being assigned to high-achieving classes.

4. The new curriculum might not match the test as well as the old curriculum. Tests measure highly specific aspects of a curriculum in highly specific ways. One study found that, three years after a district changed tests, the students did not score nearly as well on the old test as they did when it was routinely used.

5. Many tests will fall along a bell-shaped curve, but often such a curve is forced on the test-data by the test maker through the use of "item-selection techniques" and other statistical procedures. Many educators strive to make scores fall along a curve that looks like this,

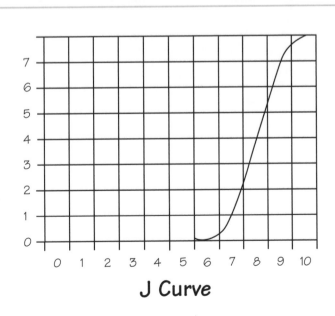

J Curve

often called a "j" curve because it resembles the letter "j." On a bell curve, most students have learned something, a few have learned a lot, and a few have learned little. On a "j" curve, most students have learned a lot, and only a few have learned little.

6. A statistically significant difference might have no practical implications. Remember that a statement of statistical significance is a statement of odds: how likely it is that the difference seen between curriculum A and curriculum B would be seen if the two curricula were really the same. (If this seems puzzling now, not to worry; this is the most technical concept in the book and will be explained in some detail.)

7. The fourth-grade student with a seventh-grade reading level has the same score as the average seventh-grader would get when reading *fourth-grade material*, not seventh-grade material.

8. Consider two students. One comes from a well-educated, affluent family and attends an elite, private, college-preparatory high school. This student scores 600 on the SAT verbal. The other student comes from an impoverished inner-city neighborhood, attends a public school with few books, has no quiet place to study, and works to help the family make ends meet. This second student also scores 600 on the SAT verbal. Are these two students equally likely to be successful in college? College admissions officers don't think so, and they're right. The student who has overcome the obstacles is a better prospect as a college student.

9. I don't think any published data exist to answer this question directly, but when I looked at scores of elementary school students over a four-year period, most students varied over that period by about 25 percentile ranks. Those above the 95th percentile varied less, but only those at the 99th percentile and those below the 10th percentile tended to have really stable scores.

10. Researchers differ wildly over the relative influence on IQ of genetics and environment. What's more, the whole question might be meaningless anyway.

CHAPTER 2

Testing, Testing, Testing

s I promised in the Introduction to this book, here are some snapshots from the contemporary testing scene.

SCENES FROM THE CURRENT WORLD OF TESTING

1. A Chicago teacher who also publishes a newspaper for teachers receives copies of the Chicago Academic Standard Examinations. He judges them atrocious. Some questions have no right answer, some questions have multiple right answers, some questions deal in stereotypes, and most questions can be called, at best, trivial pursuit items. He publishes the tests in his newspaper. The Chicago school district fires him and sues him for $1.4 million dollars, which it claims will be needed to replace the published items — items written by teachers.

2. A former teacher and test critic receives a copy of the test used by the Gwinnett County (Ga.) Public Schools. She also receives a visit from a member of the school district's police force (not a security officer) and is threatened with a felony, five years in prison, and a million dollar fine.

3. Educators in Western Massachusetts invite a well-known test critic, Alfie Kohn, to keynote a conference and title his talk "The Case Against Standardized Testing." The Massachusetts Department of Education tells the educators that, if Kohn speaks, it will yank the money to pay for the conference. The educators cave; they

pay Kohn *not* to speak. I didn't think that sort of thing was supposed to happen in this country.

4. The Virginia State Board of Education develops a set of tests as the sole determiner of school accreditation and student eligibility for high

school graduation. Various groups ask the board to permit the use of a variety of other indicators in addition to or in place of the tests. Okay, says the board — but it accepts only other kinds of tests, such as the SAT, the Advanced Placement Tests, and tests used in the International Baccalaureate program. No grades or teacher judgments of any kind — too squishy and subjective, says the board, even though the high school grade-point average still predicts success in the first year of college slightly better than does the SAT.

5. The school board in Virginia Beach, Virginia, holds a special session to decide if it should mandate recess in elementary schools. Many of the district's schools have eliminated recess and are using the time to prepare for the state's tests. An article by Associated Press reporter Gregg Toppo shows that the shortening or elimination of recess is a national phenomenon.

6. Three thousand children in New York City are erroneously forced to attend summer school after Harcourt Educational Measurement, the publisher of the test they took, mis-scores their tests. Children around the country suffer similar punishments from similar mistakes.

7. Steven Orel, a teacher in Birmingham, Alabama, points out that the city schools had expelled 522 of their lowest-scoring students just before the administration of the state test. Mr. Orel suggests the city wanted to look good. For his efforts, he is fired.

8. Author Nicholas Lemann writes a pretty large book arguing that the SAT has become the sole determiner of who gains admission to the "meritocracy." I don't think he's right. My review of *The Big Test* in the *Washington Post* is reprinted at the end of this book (p. 91-94).

9. A group of schools in New York City develops programs that use a variety of performance tests (defined later in this book) including portfolios as means of assessing their students' progress.

They want to use these assessments in place of the state-developed multiple-choice tests. No can do, says Richard Mills, New York State Commissioner of Education. They have to take the tests just like everyone else, even though their curriculum was aimed elsewhere.

10. Encouraged by teachers and some administrators, parents and students in high-scoring Scarsdale, New York, boycott the state tests. Parents had earlier complained that the district's rich curriculum was being narrowed because of time devoted to drills for the test. Commissioner Mills issues a "sharp rebuke" to the schools, ordering them to punish students if they boycott the tests again in the spring of 2002. E-mails on a test reform listserv fly back and forth under the heading "NY Commissioner has gone mad!"

THE RISE OF TESTING

Given these examples of overreliance on tests, it is hard to believe that it was not until the mid 1970s that people started paying a lot of attention to test scores. True, Banesh Hoffman had written *The Tyranny of Testing* in 1962, but his book railed more about the unfairness of a certain kind of question (multiple-choice items, which Hoffman thought penalized creative minds) than about the despotic rule of testing over education.

Few states had testing programs until the 1970s. There were no minimum-competency tests for high school graduation (except in Denver) until the late 1970s.

In 1963, scores on the SAT were just beginning to decline, and only college applicants, high school counselors, and college admissions officers were paying any attention to SAT scores at all. The National Assessment of Educational Progress (NAEP, pronounced "Nape") was still just a gleam in Ralph Tyler's eye (Tyler would serve as NAEP's principal developer). People had no international comparisons to show how U.S. test scores stacked up against those in other nations. And no one would have dreamed of giving a "readiness" test to see if children were ready for kindergarten.

Today, as we saw in "Scenes from the Current World of Testing," tests are everywhere. And they are increasingly used as weapons rather than as tools.

Just how important tests have become can be seen in how many reporters attended the press conference at the release of the results of the Third International Mathematics and Science Study (TIMSS). Educators consider themselves lucky if more than 10 reporters come to a press conference on most educational topics. But at the TIMSS press conference in November 1996, 300 people showed up. There was barely enough space along the back wall of the room — a hotel ballroom — to accommodate all the television cameras. In spite of the fact that the "news" was not very exciting — American kids were slightly above average in science, slightly below average in math — the story made the front page of the *New York Times*, the *Washington Post*, *USA Today*, and probably most papers around the nation.

Tests are so ubiquitous that, although people pay attention to the scores, they seldom ask whether the tests themselves are any good or what the scores really mean. People have come to accept tests without questioning their accuracy or appropriateness. No one at the TIMSS press conference, least of all the media, asked if you can develop a test that is equally fair to students in 41 different nations, the number participating in TIMSS. If foreign students score higher on tests, that must mean that their schools are better (it doesn't). If SAT scores are falling, that must mean that school quality is declining (it doesn't).

Unfortunately, the increased use and reporting of tests has rarely been accompanied by increased understanding of how tests ought to be used. For instance, it seems that every few years some school board member or legislator proposes a resolution urging increases in test scores so that all of the children are above average.

Of course, such a condition exists only in Lake Wobegon, the mythical Minnesota town invented by radio raconteur Garrison Keillor. In Lake

> Tests are so ubiquitous that, although people pay attention to the scores, they seldom ask whether the tests themselves are any good or what the scores really mean.

Wobegon, "all the women are strong, all the men are good looking, and all the children are above average." And it is possible for all the children in Lake Wobegon to be above average. Most of the students in rich school districts are above average. And there are ways of developing tests that could permit everyone in the country to be above average, but these ways are not used. By the conventions most commonly employed in test construction, half the children will be below average all the time. More on this point later.

People seem to have forgotten that a test is like a hammer: it is a tool with a purpose. A hammer is used to drive nails. In a pinch, it can also serve as a doorstop or a paperweight. But it has decided disadvantages as a fly swatter. Tests, too, have appropriate uses and definite limitations.

We could also liken tests to cars. Different cars are useful for different things. A station wagon or a van serves well to cart a family around, but neither is much good for racing or for getting good gas mileage. A sports car may be a lot of fun, but it's certainly not practical for a large family. Driving an SUV as if it were a Ferrari is outright dangerous.

Frederick Kelly at the University of Kansas invented the multiple-choice item in 1915. It allowed tests to take their modern form and permitted the mass testing of recruits during World War I. The sole purpose of the tests was to make discriminations among people, as opposed to, say, measuring

> Tests have been largely imposed by agencies external to schools. Teachers receive little training in analyzing tests or understanding the results.

how much people had learned in a given high school course. The early testers wanted to discriminate among people in order to make predictions about their performance later: Who would make a good tank driver, or a good gunnery officer and who would be relegated to mere cannon fodder? In the ensuing years, tests have come to be used for many other purposes, often, unfortunately, without anyone having given much thought to whether or not the new purposes were legitimate, fair, or even useful.

TESTING, THE UNREGULATED INDUSTRY

Although the testing industry is enormous, it has never been the subject of any investigation, and it is largely unregulated. About a decade ago, a group of educators and civil rights activists who were dissatisfied with test use in general and with the Educational Testing Service (ETS), in particular, founded the National Center for Fair and Open Testing, usually referred to simply as FairTest (www.fairtest.org).

Begun as an anti-SAT, anti-ETS organization, FairTest has expanded its horizons. It has for some years called attention to such issues as the gender bias of tests. Recently, it reviewed the testing programs of all states and evaluated them on a scale of 1 (needs complete overhaul) to 5 (model program). There were many 1s and few 5s. But FairTest is nowhere near being a Consumer's Union of testing, able to publish a monthly *Consumer Reports* or a *Test Buyer's Guide* the way Consumer's Union

publishes its widely read magazine and its series of buyer's guides.

More recently, George Madaus and others at Boston College established the National Board on Educational Testing and Public Policy (www.nbetpp.bc.edu). This board

- monitors testing programs, policies, and products;
- evaluates the benefits and costs of testing programs in operation; and
- assesses the extent to which professional standards for test development and use are met in practice.

It is too soon to tell what, if any, impact, this board will have. Some observers are predicting that it will not last. When the concept was first developed, even test companies expressed support, but they have abandoned it in their quest for profits — the U.S. spends about $400,000,000 a year on testing. Currently, any concerns about professional standards are swamped by concerns about profits and political expediency. In short, the politicians want tests, and they are willing to let taxpayers pay from them.

The *Mental Measurements Yearbook* (which is actually published every few years) reviews tests, but these reviews are by testing specialists, and they are primarily directed at other testing specialists. Most of them accept the state of testing pretty much as it is, and most of them would be incomprehensible to lay readers because they assume that review readers know the jargon of testing (of which there is plenty).

In free-market economics, one principle quickly emerges: markets work only when consumers have easy access to accurate, reliable information about the products they wish to purchase. Such information about tests has not been readily available. Of course, most people never "buy" a test directly, and that exacerbates the problem of secrecy and lack of information. Indeed, most tests that people take are imposed on them or their children by some agency, such as a school district or a state or a college admissions office that requires SAT or ACT scores.

Parents whose children are given tests need to know what the tests can and cannot say about children. They need to be able to evaluate whether or not the decisions made about their children on the basis of test scores are fair and appropriate. Teachers need similar information, especially if the tests are used not only to evaluate the children, but also to judge the teachers' own performance. Administrators need to know about tests to determine what policy decisions about the district — and the administrators in it — are appropriate.

Why don't parents, teachers, and school administrators have all of the information they need? After all, don't educators make use of all the information generated by these tests? In fact, most of the people who work in school buildings do not make much use of tests at all. Tests have been largely imposed by agencies external to schools. Teachers receive little training in analyzing tests or understanding the results. Test companies are all private corporations, and the information about their tests is proprietary—they only have to tell you what they want to.

Tests were developed by people who came to be known as psychometricians, literally, people who measure psychological traits. Teachers have always regarded tests as alien inventions or interesting curiosities, even when they have borrowed the dominant multiple-choice format.

People began to change their relaxed view of tests in October 1957, my senior year in high school. The short answer to why tests became so important is that people lost confidence in their schools and the people who ran them. Let us see how and why that happened.

THE HISTORICAL CONTEXT

After World War II, school policy makers saw schools for the first time as integral to national defense. We became locked in weapons and space races with the Communist powers, and Americans looked to schools to provide the mathematicians, scientists, and engineers needed to win. Some, like Adm. Hyman Rickover and CIA chief Allen

Dulles, contended that the schools were not up to the task, and criticism of the schools, always abundant, increased.

In October 1957, the Russians launched Sputnik, the first man-made satellite. To the school critics, Sputnik proved that they had been right all along. The critics' recipe for higher achievement at this time was not to test children, but to provide them with new, improved curricula. Some of the finest minds at universities such as Yale and Stanford built these curricula, and people had high hopes for them. Unfortunately, these fine minds had no experience with schools and, indeed, tried to circumvent them. During this period, the phrase "teacher-proof" became common. But, by ignoring the people in the schools — not to mention ignoring how people learn — the brainy curriculum makers virtually guaranteed that their products would fail, and they mostly did.

The schools never recovered from Sputnik. In a marvelous little 1989 book, *Popular Education and Its Discontents,* the distinguished education historian Lawrence Cremin observed that after World War II both secondary education and college education experienced unprecedented expansions. But he also observed that "this expansion was accompanied by a pervasive sense of failure. The question would have to be, why?"

That is, indeed, the question. And, aside from the national defense concerns cited above, there really is no rational answer save to say that the public schools can always be improved and that they are easy targets because they are so public and because the typical reaction of school people to criticism is to work harder, not to defend themselves. In 1970, journalist Charles Silberman observed that, of nearly 200 studies comparing scores on tests at two different times, virtually all favored the more recent point in history. Yet Silberman titled his book *Crisis in the Classroom.*

For those worried about the quality of the schools, the question became, "If we can't trust the people in the schools to tell us about how well the schools

> There is a critical need for clear information about what tests can and cannot do, about how they are constructed, and about how they are used and misused.

are doing, what can we trust?" In looking around for means by which to evaluate schools, various outsiders discovered tests.

Tests were external. Tests were objective. Best of all, tests in their multiple-choice formats were cheap. And once answer sheets could be scored electronically, the results could be known quickly.

The importance of testing also increased as the result of a committee convened in 1976 by the College Entrance Examination Board. The College Board assigned the committee the task of analyzing what was then a 13-year decline in scores on the Scholastic Aptitude Test (then the name of the SAT). The committee attributed much of the decline to changes in who was going to college: more women, more minorities, and more students with low grade-point averages. It also fingered the cultural events of the late Sixties and early Seventies as potential causes: the civil rights movement, the women's movement, the formation of a counter culture, the recreational use of drugs, urban riots, Watergate, and Vietnam, all of which functioned together to create what the committee called "a decade of distraction."

The committee's conclusions, though, were not those routinely reported in the media and, thus, not those of the public. The committee had asked, "What has caused the SAT decline?" The committee had answered, "A large number of factors,

acting together in complex ways." Not interested in complexity or subtlety, the media — and the public — attributed the slump to a deterioration in the quality of high schools.

The report also drew a great deal of attention to the SAT, and each tiny change in scores each year became front-page news. The SAT's principal developer had referred to it as a "mere supplement" to the rest of the high school record. Now it had become for some, a platinum rod for measuring schools.

In the alarm surrounding the decline in SAT scores, new uses for tests appeared. Suddenly, there were tests for basic skills, for high school graduation, for teacher certification, and for accountability.

The SAT decline continued until 1983. In that year a "paper Sputnik" was launched with the publication of *A Nation at Risk*. This report of the National Commission on Excellence in Education opened with Cold War rhetoric about how, if an unfriendly foreign power imposed our schools on us, we would consider it an act of war. The booklet "proved" its conclusions with selected, spun, and distorted statistics. Still, *Risk* became the launching pad both for new anxieties about schools and for new efforts to reform them. Many of those reforms called for increased use of tests.

I refer to *Risk* as "the little blue book of propaganda." A 1997 story in the *New York Times* stated that most experts now consider *Risk* as only very good propaganda. Many who want to increase "accountability" in schools, though, still invoke the report as a "landmark study." It was more a land mine than a landmark.

Results from international studies have also increased anxiety about schools: we're not number one. In fact, TIMSS, the largest comparison of test scores among countries, generated a new cliché among some school critics: the longer American students stay in school, the dumber they get compared to their peers in other developed nations. This is not true, as we shall see later, but the

TIMSS results generated even more interest in test scores.

There is, then, a critical need for clear information about what tests can and cannot do, about how they are constructed, and about how they are used and misused. It is my hope that this book will prove to be a source of such information.

CONCERNS ABOUT TECHNICAL TERMS

Teachers construct classroom tests with none of the formal item-tryouts and committee review and statistics associated with the construction of commercial tests. They are means of representing teachers' judgments about how well students are performing. Once we leave the realm of classroom assessments, though, we enter a new domain full of statistics and technical terms. We cannot avoid them if we are to fully understand tests.

And, increasingly, people need to understand tests. In 1997, I testified in a lawsuit to determine whether or not a particular school district could or could not use a test to retain students in grade. While much of the testimony presented evidence that retention in grade does not work well, another line of argument turned on the fact that the test's "standard error of measurement" was too large for the school to use the test in promotion/retention decisions. Other expert witnesses and I pointed out that, given a particular "observed score," a student's "true score" could easily exceed the "cut score" needed for promotion. While we tried to talk in plain English and not in formulas, we did have to define all of the terms in quotes above in hopes of helping the judge understand our arguments.

Similarly, scores on Virginia's Standards of Learning tests are arranged along a scale from zero to 600. A student who obtains a 400 or better passes the test; a student who gets "only" 399 fails. This appearance of precision is false. A one-point difference between success and failure on this scale is ridiculous. Given the error of measurement, it is estimated that, as of the end of the 2000-2001 school year, the test had misclassified half a million Virginia students: they will have failed when they should have passed or passed when they should have failed.

As tests assume more and more visibility as a means of holding students, teachers, and others accountable for school outcomes, the technical terms of testing will become increasingly used in the popular culture, and so you will need some familiarity with them. In this book, these terms have been placed toward the back of the book so that they do not impede readers who are mostly interested in types of tests and how they are used. Refer to them as needed or skip to Chapter 6, "Interpreting Test Scores," to become familiar with them and keep them in mind as you read the rest of the book.

CHAPTER 3

Standardized Tests, Social Policy, and the Purpose of Education

We will deal with specific uses of tests in the next chapter, but first we must discuss a general concern with regard to the issue of test use. Tests in this country have historically been used to sort people: officers and enlisted men; college material and vocational school material; the gifted and talented and the rest of us; bluebirds and robins. In fact, the schools themselves have sometimes been called "The Great Sorting Machine." Some people argue that sorting is a fundamental *purpose* of schools — to get people into the appropriate societal slots. Others argue that the schools should educate all children to the highest possible levels. Both positions have had prominent followers, and the debates between advocates of the two positions have been heated, to say the least.

Today, universal (almost) free public education is available to all who want it through 12th grade, and relatively inexpensive public colleges provide tertiary education at a reasonable price. Community colleges are even cheaper. Today, the sorting takes place within the schools. The most obvious use of testing as a sorting device occurs in tracking wherein some students are permitted to study more advanced topics than are other students. Because such tracking has obvious lifelong effects on people and because such tracking decisions are fallible, many people now oppose the practice. (Many of the opponents also have a fundamentally different belief about the nature of human intelligence, discussed below.)

The early testers saw tracking as humane: to confront a child of low ability with the same curricu-

lum as provided to a child of high ability would only frustrate and humiliate the student with lower ability. This attitude exists in many places today although its expression is often muted because in the tenor of these times it is not "politically correct." And, in fact, it might also be wrong. The issue is much debated.

Even more muted is a belief among some that more resources should be allocated to more able students because it is from this group that society will get the biggest return on its investment. Few are willing to voice this belief because of its obviously elitist stance. Charles Murray, co-author of *The Bell Curve* and one of the few willing to take this stance in public, contends, "Just because it's elitist doesn't make it wrong."

For others, the purpose of education is to assist *all* children to be all that they can be. Tracking, sorting, grouping, classifying — whatever it is called — denies some students the opportunity to be other than hewers of wood and drawers of water. It therefore betrays the fundamental precepts on which America was founded.

For the record, I am enamored of a definition of education formulated by philosopher of education Israel Sheffler:

> The formation of habits of judgment and the development of character, the elevation of standards, the facilitation of understanding, the development of taste and discrimination, the stimulation of curiosity and wondering, the fostering of style and a sense of beauty, the growth of a thirst for new ideas and visions of the yet unknown.

Not exactly a test-oriented perspective.

SECRECY

If you are surprised to see a separate section on secrecy ("test security," it's usually called) because you don't think it's an issue, then your next reaction should be fear because you have been seduced into accepting as natural a most unusual, even pathological situation. In *Assessing Student Behavior,* Grant Wiggins captured the setting and our too usual casual reaction to it well:

> It is so common that we barely give it a second thought: the tests that we and others design to evaluate the success of student learning invariably depend upon secrecy. Secrecy as to the

questions that will be asked. Secrecy as to how the questions will be chosen. Secrecy as to how the results will be scored. Sometimes secrecy as to when we will be tested. Secrecy as to what the scores mean. Secrecy as to how the results will be used. What a paradoxical affair! Our aim is to educate, to prepare, to enlighten, yet our habits of testing are built upon procedures that continually keep students in the dark — procedures with roots in premodern traditions of legal proceedings and religious inquisitions.[4]

Actually, the situation is worse than that because Wiggins has only the students in mind. But most of the time the teachers don't know what is going on either. In many school testing programs, the tests are kept away from teachers until the very last minute. And teachers (and administrators) face job termination — or worse — if they are accused of tampering with the tests or the results.

Wiggins contends that secrecy in testing helps produce people who are both docile (they put up with it) and leery. The point is also made by anthropologist F. Allan Hanson in *Testing Testing: Social Consequences of the Examined Life.* "Whether the results are positive or negative is irrelevant. The point is that testing opens the self to scrutiny and investigation in ways that the self is powerless to control. So far as the areas of knowledge covered by the test are concerned, this transforms the person from autonomous subject to passive object."[5]

Both Wiggins and Hanson observe that testing increases the power of the tester over the tested and that the secrecy enhances this power differential. Wiggins likens the situation to the story of the Emperor's new clothes. Secrecy allows test makers to insist that only people with their special skills can produce tests.

The situation is not likely to improve soon. In fact, since that last sentence was written in 1997 and now, early 2002, the situation has deteriorated substantially.

THE USES (AND MISUSES) OF TESTS

This section discusses the common uses of standardized tests including those uses which are really not legitimate.

Monitoring. This is a rather informal use, made by teachers and parents alike. The tests are used as a kind of "reality check" to see if the test results for a child accord with other indicators of achievement, such as classroom performance and report card grades. Testers like to emphasize that tests are external to the classroom and "objective" — in contrast to the "subjective" judgments of teachers.

Teacher judgments are fallible, of course, but so are tests, and the teacher's "subjective" judgments are based on observing the child over a much longer period of time. Thus the tests can be misused if people put too much faith in and give too much weight to the test over the other information. And in the end tests are subjective too — some human being, some "subject" constructs them. As Alfie Kohn puts it, test results "emerge from the interaction of two sets of human beings: the invisible adults who make up the questions and the rows of kids scrunched into desks, frantically writing (or filling in bubbles)."[6]

Unfortunately, teachers have contributed to the growing faith in test results over grades because they have been guilty of "grade inflation." Perceived as unwilling to judge work by its quality or yielding to parental pressure for a higher grade, teachers have had the accuracy and worth of their grades impugned. As people came to distrust the meaning of grades they have looked to some external instrument, and usually the only one around is some kind of test. (One wonders how many parents distrust grades because they have successfully persuaded a teacher to alter some for their children.)

There is a more formal kind of monitoring in connection with accountability. In some states, schools that score low on tests are put on a list to be monitored. They need to show improvement on the tests to get off the list. If they do not improve, state actions follow. Sometimes these actions take the form of increased resources; more often they come as punishments such as loss of accreditation, transfer of a principal, etc.

Diagnosis. Few educational tests can be used to make diagnoses, no matter what the claims of the test publishers in this regard might be. First, the tests are fairly blunt instruments. Medical tests, by contrast, are aimed at specific conditions: the number of red cells, the amount of sugar in the blood, the level of cholesterol or prostate specific antigen, for example. Some results from medical tests yield prescriptions directly: too much sugar in the blood, take this pill, lose weight, exercise more, and watch your diet. Other medical test results lead to further testing to narrow down the possible problems.

Most educational tests are designed to report on more general and somewhat vaguely specified concepts: reading comprehension or mathematics computation. No prescriptions flow from their results.

Because educational tests yield general results, they contain too few items on any one skill area to give a very reliable indication at the level of the individual child. In the arena of arithmetic, there is more opportunity for diagnostic work than in other areas because the skills are more concrete and precisely defined. For instance, a math item on one test said that at one point in time, the outside temperature was 13 degrees Fahrenheit. A few hours later the temperature was 28 degrees colder. The question asked the child what the temperature was at the second time. The options:

> −15 degrees (the correct answer)
> 28 degrees (the child hasn't considered the whole question)
> 41 degrees (the child performed the wrong arithmetical operation)
> 15 degrees (the child performed the right operation but did not take the sign of the numbers into account)

If a child consistently made errors like that in answer number 4 on similar problems, we could tell that he or she needed work in the area of understanding negative numbers. Results from educational tests are seldom so specific.

Even here, though, the test is not very diagnostic and certainly not prescriptive. It tells the teacher she needs to do something, but not what to do. The best analogy might be to liken the test to a thermometer. An above normal temperature tells you that something is wrong, but, by itself, it provides no clues about what the ailment is, for many illnesses cause temperatures to rise. Without a diagnosis, there can be no prescription for a cure.

Teacher Accountability. This is one of the most seductive uses of tests because, at first glance, it seems so reasonable. Of course a teacher should be accountable for what her students know.

Unfortunately, the situation is not so simple. There are a variety of problems with using tests for teacher accountability. In the first place, one teacher might emphasize what is on the test while another prefers to teach other subject matter and can provide good justifications for doing so. Teachers can't teach everything (although they sometimes try), and two teachers may well differ on what to teach or how to teach the same material. One could elect to teach science through physics; another, through ecology. One could elect to present science as a series of disciplines; another could emphasize science as a process, focusing on the scientific method that cuts across disciplines.

In addition, there are always more topics in a textbook than on a test. Because of their length, tests can never measure everything that's taught. So students will learn some topics that are not tested. And some material on the test will not have been taught. Finally, according to psychometrician W. James Popham, there are items on tests that students learn outside of school. More than you'd think, Popham claims. This, of course, gives an advantage to students from privileged backgrounds.

> Tests can be misused if people put too much faith in and give too much weight to the test over the other information.

Of course, if the tests *are* used for high-stakes accountability, teachers *will* come to emphasize what is on them. Perhaps the most vivid instance of teachers aligning their instruction to the test occurred in suburban Prince George's County, Maryland, in the 1980s. A new superintendent, John Murphy, arrived, as most new superintendents do, announcing goals and promises for the district. One was get test scores up overall and to close the gap between the scores of black students and white students. Murphy established one room in the administration building as his "applied anxiety room." The room's walls held charts showing test score trends for each school.

Over time, test scores rose. And the ethnic gap, while it did not vanish, narrowed substantially. Black students, who constitute about 65% of the children in the Prince George's system, were scoring comfortably above the national norm.

But some of us heard stories that instruction in some Prince George's schools looked a lot like getting ready to take a test. Children would go to the blackboard and select one of four or five preselected answers to a problem or question. And so forth. Several organizations requested permission to conduct external evaluations of the programs. Murphy refused. The state of Maryland used this test for more years than it should have, but it finally adopted a new test. Often, when a new test is brought into a state, scores go down. New item formats, new content, and other differences, all operate to lower scores a bit. The year that

Maryland adopted the new test, scores went down all over the state. The drop was more noticeable than usual, probably because the state had used the old test so long. But in Prince George's County the scores did not just fall, they plummeted, some scores for black students falling as low as the 18th percentile. Fortunately for Murphy, he had already taken a job in another state.

There are other problems with using tests for teacher accountability. For instance, the process collides with the common system of teacher assignment. Logically, one might think that schools would send the best teachers into the toughest classes. But schools don't have many ways to reward teachers. Lacking tangible compensations, administrators often reward their perception of good teaching by sending the good teachers to high-achieving classes. High test scores for one teacher might reflect good teaching, but they might also reflect the prior achievement of the students or the socioeconomic status of the students' parents.

Children do not arrive in a classroom as blank slates. They come with previous levels of achievement. These levels of achievement depend greatly on what happens and has happened outside of school. Even George Will, the conservative pundit and school critic, has acknowledged that from birth to age 18, an American child is in school only 9% of the time. The external environment thus affects test scores a great deal. The Kane and Staiger study mentioned earlier raises new concerns about using test scores in accountability schemes, especially if the accountability system uses annual score changes: such changes are highly volatile, and most of the change is associated with factors other than teaching.

Finally, 20% of American students change schools each year. In urban areas, the percentage is much higher. In some accountability systems, teachers might be accountable for students they have taught for only a short time.

It would be better to follow a specific group of students through school. That is, we should look at the test scores of the same children as they move through the grades. In some districts, though, the mobility rate is so high that only a few children would be left at the end of just a few years.

A rational approach to the use of tests as accountability devices for teachers might be to test the children in the fall and use these test scores and a variety of demographic variables to predict test scores at the end of the year. The end-of-year scores could then be matched against the predictions. It would be necessary, of course, to ensure that the test actually reflected what had been — or should have been — taught during the year.

For all its apparent rationality, though, fall-to-spring testing often produces misleading results. If people know they are being evaluated on fall-to-spring changes, they can act to depress test results in the fall. It's not that hard. In addition, low-income students suffer greater "summer loss" than their more affluent peers. The gains of spring do not hold up into the following fall. (In general, middle class students continue to gain in reading scores and their math scores are stable. Low-income students show declines in both subjects.)

Using testing for accountability also runs smack into a human foible: people strive to make themselves look good. Period. When organizations started rating airlines on the percentage of on-time arrivals, the times to fly from one place to another suddenly got longer. Airlines built a lot of "fudge time" into their schedules. (I travel a lot, and it is often the case that we arrive early and then sit on the tarmac waiting for an open gate).

People should be wary about attempts to use tests to make schools or districts look good. One district gamed the system by administering a test to students in the fall and again in the spring but scoring the test both times using the spring norms. The spring norms reflect growth from fall to spring. The students might not look so good in the fall, but the school will be able to show a lot of growth by spring. This would be true even if the children didn't learn much during the year.

Principal/Superintendent/Board Accountability.
There are states such as Michigan and North
Carolina, where the consequences of low test
scores are visited not upon the teachers but upon
one or more of the school's or district's administrators. These programs are too new to know what
actual impact they will have. In North Carolina, if
a school is declared low achieving, it receives
assistance from the state, and its principal is put on
probation. In one instance where this happened in
1997, the district sued the state. The district won,
and the principal was reinstated.

All the considerations mentioned under teacher
accountability apply here as well. There are various
ways of predicting test scores that take into
account the demographic conditions of a school.
One method is to compare a particular school to
other schools with similar demographics. This
method was used in California for some years.
Some schools were unhappy about what the state
considered "comparable schools," but, since there
were no real sanctions attached, the issue was not
pressed. North Carolina uses the other major tech-
nique, using the school's demographics to set
growth targets and then using test scores to see if
the targets have been achieved. But, as noted, the
programs are too new to be evaluated for their full
ramifications.

Student Accountability. There is a growing trend
in this country to base decisions regarding grade
promotion, retention in grade, or high school
graduation on test scores.

About retention in grade, this needs to be said:
it seldom works. Study after study has found the
consequences to be negative. One study ranked 49
educational innovations in terms of their impact on
achievement. Retention in grade ranked 49th. It
was among the few innovations that actually produced *negative* results.

Why do people believe that retention works?
Largely because they are not in a position to conduct a controlled experiment. (There are teachers,
too, who take a moral position on retaining a low-

achieving child, independent of the academic
impact.) Teachers and parents watch the retained
child in the second year in a grade. Most children
do better the second time around, but not a whole
lot better. Few bloom into high achievers. Parents
and teachers who observe a child struggling in the
same grade a second year then assume that the
child's difficulties would have been that much
worse if the child had been promoted.

But, for a variety of reasons, there have been
occasions when some low-achieving children
were retained and others with the same low
achievement were promoted. The next year, the
promoted children did as well as or better than
their retained peers.

Flunking kids is often presented as the only alternative to "social promotion" or promotion for "seat
time." When policy makers and politicians make
this claim, they are being expedient at best. When
teachers or administrators make this claim, they are
simultaneously making a stunning admission of
incompetence. All of these groups are also left with
nothing to say when confronted with the high-
achieving schools of Japan and Scandinavia,
schools that practice neither retention nor tracking
prior to high school. Obviously, there are other
ways to get the job done.

But we must assume that educators will go on
retaining children. At the 1996 "Education
Summit," Bill Clinton declared himself against
"social promotion." In the fall of 1997, so did the
American Federation of Teachers. Will tests help in
deciding who should stay back? Possibly, but often
not. They will be of extremely limited use if the
child has only taken the test once. And, unfortunately, this is sometimes the case. Students in Chicago
have been forced to attend summer school or be
retained in grade on the basis of a single administration of the Iowa Tests of Basic Skills — a use for
which the ITBS was never intended. Students in
New York City have suffered similar fates.

Indeed, no matter what decisions flow from tests,
children should be afforded the opportunity to take

the test more than once. The American Educational Research Association, the American Psychological Association, and the National Council for Measurement in Education — the three major professional organizations working with educational tests — jointly issued standards for test use. Among these is the standard that a single test should never be used alone to make important decisions about an individual or a group. Multiple measures afford different perspectives. Some students ace multiple-choice tests and freeze on performance tests. For other students, the reverse holds. It is important — indeed, crucial — to have multiple types of measures and multiple results from the same measure. The recent position statement of the American Educational Research Association on high-stakes testing is germane here and is included in the back of this book.

Recall we earlier said that no test is a perfect measure. All tests contain measurement error. If we make decisions based on a single test administered at a single time, we run a large risk of making the wrong decision. When we administer the same test to the students more than once, our chances of making a mistake are reduced. If a student gets, say, three shots at a test and fails it all three times, the chances that he got a low score by chance are much smaller (but not zero) than if he had only one opportunity to take the test.

Selection Decisions. As noted in the beginning, tests were designed to discriminate among people in order to provide some people one set of educational experiences (officers' candidate school, college entry, a more challenging curriculum, etc.), and other people different educational experiences. The hope has always been to match the experiences to people's needs and abilities, but it has not always worked out that way.

In selecting students for college, admissions officers have a great deal of information about students beyond SAT (or ACT) scores, grades, and rank in class. Many colleges now ask for essays, and students themselves sometimes send in videotapes. By now, they might well be sending software for the dean to download (perhaps with a virus that activates if the dean rejects the student?). As noted in the chapter on specific tests, schools that have abandoned the SAT have experienced positive changes in both the students who apply for admission and those who actually come.

Currently, almost half the students who start college don't finish. This was true when I matriculated in 1958, but society's attitude about it is different now. And the 50% figure is misleading. I recall the dean of men at the public college I attended proudly announcing at the first fall convocation that 50% of us would not make it. He saw the 50% figure as evidence that the college upheld its standards. Currently, people view it with alarm as a "dropout rate."

The figure is misleading because, when I was in college, we did not have our community college system. College completion rates are now much higher at my college and similar four-year institutions. The "dropout rate" from community colleges greatly exceeds 50%, but, of course, some of these "dropouts" have simply tried college and decided it wasn't for them.

In any case, the admissions process, tests and all, is not highly accurate. The SAT accounts for only 20% of the variability in freshman grades. That means that 80% of what determinees who makes Dean's List and who gets socked with academic probation comes from other factors.

Actually, as many observers have pointed out, few colleges are "selecting" students. From 1977 to 1994, the number of high school graduates declined each year in the wake of the baby boom. Yet college enrollments rose by over 4,000,000 during the same period. Instead of cutting faculty, staff, and programs as the number of high school graduates declined, many colleges shifted from selecting students to recruiting them. I recall my two children, good but not exceptional students in high school, receiving lots of glossy, full color brochures touting the virtues of various colleges. It is still true that only about one applicant in seven gets admitted to schools like Amherst, Brown, and Harvard, but these elite schools are few in number.

With the secondary school population now growing, and the proportion of high school graduates aiming for college continuing to rise, colleges have become more selective, but not in comparison to what they were in the 1960s.

In selecting students for gifted and talented programs or other enrichment programs, tests often play a dominant role — sometimes the only role. Occasionally, a group-administered IQ test serves as the criterion; more often a commercial achievement test is used. Typically, a certain percentile is used as a cut score. Some room is left for teacher nomination and parental pressure as well. In districts with diverse populations, the administration sometimes resorts to a percentage of students rather than percentile. The top, say, 5% of test scorers are selected into the program, allowing all schools to have similar-sized programs. Naturally, the schools in the more affluent parts of the district protest because some students excluded in these schools would qualify in a less affluent school.

Selection into special education programs does not usually depend so heavily on tests. This is good because the tests used for diagnosis of special needs, while specialized, often are not as reliable as the typical achievement tests. Decisions for special education selection are made, or at least should be, in a group consultation involving teachers, parents, and the special education specialists of the district.

STANDARDS AND HIGH-STAKES TESTING

Nothing illustrates the shift from tests-as-tools to tests-as-juggernauts better than the rise of the standards-and-testing movement. Because of its dominance in talk about schools today, it deserves a separate discussion.

First, we have to define *standard* because the word has many meanings: standard equipment, standard excuse, standard grade of meat, standard temperature and pressure, platinum standard (for measur-

> If we make decisions based on a single test administered at a single time, we run a large risk of making the wrong decision.

ing length, etc.), and so on. None of these captures the meaning of standard in education today and, indeed, some confuse standard with standardization. *The American Heritage Dictionary* gives as synonyms for standard "benchmark, criterion, gauge, measure, touchstone, or yardstick." And it notes that "the central meaning shared by these nouns is 'a point of reference against which individuals are compared and evaluated.'" That's what those advocating standards mean today.

The concern with standards in American education is one of long standing. In the May 1914 issue of the *American School Board Journal,* Assistant New York City Superintendent Andrew Edson, wrote that "many maintain that the three R's and formal drill are neglected, that the work of pupils and teachers, owing to the fads and frills which are included, is superficial and that promotions from grade to grade are made without much regard to real attainments" (p. 11).

In the era leading up to World War II, schools became engulfed in the cult of efficiency. During this time, raising standards mostly meant saving money or time. Schools and groups outside of schools did indeed use a "school survey" to rank schools or compare one to another, but the standards had little to do with curriculum or instruction. Teachers were rated on their general appearance, health, optimism, and the like and on how well they managed light, heat, and ventilation. Students were largely ignored in the surveys.

After World War II, this changed. We were locked in a Cold War with the Soviet Union. Schools and the "products" coming out of them were now seen as integral to national defense. In its March 24, 1958 edition, *Life* began a five-part series on the "Crisis in Education." The "crisis" had come to light as a consequence of the Soviet Union's launch of Sputnik, the first man-made satellite. Describing the series, the editors observed that "the standards of education are shockingly low" (p. 25). This sentiment has been expressed many times in the ensuing years.

In 1963, U.S. Commissioner of Education Francis Keppel[7] observed that "it has often been pointed out that America lacks standards by which it can measure educational results, and stimulate its students to greater accomplishment. One means to solve this national problem is to work out ways of taking samples of the achievement of students at critical points in their school." These musings led Keppel to develop the National Assessment of Educational Progress which is given its own section on pages 56-59.

Keppel's thinking represents the modern position of standards advocates: we can set a standard and then develop a test to measure where students are in respect to that standard. Actually, this conceptualization harks back to a credo put forward in 1918 by Edward Thorndike, one of the founders of the testing movement: "If something exists, it exists in some amount." That is, anything can be quantified.

There is no indication that Keppel thought that measuring "educational results" should lead to sanctions. But others did. In the 1970s, the nation went through a craze for "minimum competency testing." Minimum competency tests determined whether or not a student would get a diploma from high school. Problems with minimum competency tests are discussed on pages 35-36 in the section on Criterion-Referenced Tests. After *A Nation at Risk* appeared in 1983, concern rose for the other end of the achievement spectrum. After all, the group that produced *Risk* was the National Commission on

Excellence in Education. It wrote, "We should expect schools to have genuinely high standards rather than minimum ones."

The Reagan Administration and first Bush Administration, in power from 1980 to 1992, pushed many federal initiatives back to the states. One consequence of this policy in education was that states began developing lists of what students should know (standards) and how that knowledge should be demonstrated — through tests.

And if the students failed to show the "right" amount of knowledge? The results could be summer school, retention in grade, and failure to graduate. "Right" is in quotes because the setting of "cut scores" to determine how much achievement is enough has been capricious. The Virginia Board of Education, for instance, obtained about 20 recommended cut scores for each test, then accepted *only* the highest — except in two cases where it actually set the cut scores higher than anyone had recommended. In California, the process was even more dicey. Delaine Easton, the state superintendent, decided she didn't like the cut scores recommended by her committee so she lowered them. In Massachusetts, a state that performs very well on NAEP, zero percent of fourth-graders managed to obtain the status of "advanced" on the state reading test.

In light of the ludicrously high cut scores and the attached sanctions, teachers began to devote even more time to what the tests contained. Recess shortened or disappeared altogether. Curriculum areas not covered by the tests also disappeared. Many young children threw up on test day, and a few suicides were recorded. All this in the name of maintaining high standards. The warrior-like approach of standards advocates was such that in *One Size Fits Few: The Folly of Educational Standards,* writer and teacher Susan Ohanian gave them a name. She called them Standardistos.

High-stakes testing raises the issue of fairness in two ways. First, there is the general question: Is it fair to any student to require, by law, that he or she attend something called school for 12 years — the alternative is jail — and then deny that student a diploma based on a test?

Second, we know very well that black and Hispanic students do not score as well on tests as white students. The average black high school senior scores about as high on the NAEP reading and mathematics tests as the average white eighth-grader. In science, black seniors are significantly behind white eighth-graders. The high-stakes *testing* programs do not come with the resources to ameliorate these differences. Standards proponents, such as Diane Ravitch of New York University and E. D. Hirsch, Jr., of the University of Virginia, have argued that standards programs will eliminate the "achievement gap" between whites and minorities. So far, the programs have only made the disparities greater.

In late 2001, a group of about a dozen testing experts were convened by five large educational organizations to make testing, especially high-stakes testing, more relevant to instruction.[8] This Commission on Instructionally Supportive Assessment, prepared a set of nine requirements that, it hopes, will ensure that tests do support instruction.

The report of this commission notes that states often create more standards than can possibly be taught in a year. Given this, state tests concentrate on the standards most easily assessed. These tests also "rarely provide educators with the kind of information they need to improve instruction."

It is too early to tell how the "requirements" for instructionally supportive assessment will mesh with the new Bush Administration's legislation or what impact, if any, the report will have on anyone.

FACTORS INFLUENCING TEST SCORES

Discussions about tests in the media often make it seem as if only the school has any influence on them. This is hardly true. After all, a child only spends 9% of his or her life from birth to age 18 in school.

Incredibly, many states ignore obvious influences on schools. In mid-September 2001, the state of Colorado announced which of its schools had received the labels of "excellent" and "unsatisfactory" (there are three other categories as well). The labels come from the test scores on the Colorado Student Assessment Program. An "analysis" of these results by the *Rocky Mountain News* found that the "unsatisfactory" schools had high percentages of minority students living in poverty. The dropout rates for these schools were seven times what they were for the excellent schools. The excellent schools were virtually all white, and virtually none of their students lived in poverty. What a surprise.

We should keep the following factors in mind when thinking about test scores:

Family Income. If you look at the College Board's *Profiles of College-Bound Seniors,* which comes out each fall with the release of SAT scores, you will see a table showing SAT scores by income level. There is a very clear progression—the higher the income, the higher the SAT. I tell audiences that given only a set of test scores, I know more about the socioeconomic status of the community than anything else.

Parental Education. Measures of "socioeconomic status" mentioned in the last paragraph usually include some measure of parents' education. In many studies, the parents' educational level is the single biggest factor contributing to the test scores of children. Incidentally, the educational level of Asian Americans is much higher than that of the country as a whole.

Poverty. One study examined scores in high- and low-poverty schools. High-poverty schools were defined as those in which at least 76% of the students were eligible for free or reduced-price lunches. Low-poverty schools had zero to 20% eligibility rates. The researchers first divided the students into groups depending on the kinds of letter grades they took home on report cards. Then they looked to see how these groups performed on standardized tests of reading and math. Students in low-poverty schools who got A's scored about as you would expect, averaging the 81st percentile in reading and the 87th in math. Students in high poverty schools who got A's scored higher than their peers who got lower grades, but in neither case did the average score reach even the 40th percentile.

It is popular these days for conservative organizations to seek out high-poverty schools that also have high test scores. These organizations then imply that because not all similar schools score as high, public education has failed. *No Excuses* was the title of such a report from the Heritage Foundation. On close examination, one finds that these high-poverty schools are exceptional in many ways. They have principals who are willing to work 100 hours a week and demand the same of their teachers. They often have 11-month school years, longer school days, and courses after school and on Saturdays. They are often small schools with small classes, two factors known to improve achievement. We can applaud these schools and the dedicated people who operate them, but as one of them said, to do this nationwide would require a whole new species of educator. In addition, it must be said, some of the high test scores reported in these schools were so high that we can be certain they are not real.

Motivation. Motivation can have an enormous impact on scores. A true story:

> When I was director of testing for the state of Virginia, tests had become so important to the public image of the schools that the districts were employing a significant number of what the state superintendent referred to as "inappropriate administrative procedures" — cheating to the rest of us.

> We devised a computer program to detect unusual patterns of changes in test scores. One year, the computer spit out the name of a small, rural district, and in our role as police-

men, we visited the superintendent to figure out what had happened. Although located in a rural area, the district was located near enough to some suburban districts that its score appeared in the same newspaper. The inevitable comparisons were not favorable to the rural district.

> The superintendent told us that most of the students in the district were not going to college. They would be going to work on their parents' farms or in farm-related industries. Most of them knew pretty much what they would be doing when they finished high school. The tests played no role in their future and, therefore, the superintendent said, "They don't take these tests seriously."

> To make students more serious about the tests, the superintendent decided to take them out of the academic arena. He presented the tests, not as an opportunity for the students to show how smart they were or how well their teachers had taught them, but as a chance to beat their archrivals in the adjacent county, just as they tried to do each year in football, basketball, and baseball. And it was true that, if you asked a student in these schools what they were going to do with the tests, they would say "Beat _____ County!" (naming the neighboring county).

> During the week of testing, the teachers dressed as cheerleaders and led pep rallies in the auditorium, where the students in the affected grades were cheered on by their non-tested peers. The motivational program worked. Depending on age and test topic, the scores that the computer found suspicious were 15 to 30 percentile ranks higher than the previous year's marks.

Personal Hygiene. I use this term to cover things like getting a good night's sleep before the day of testing and eating well on the day of testing. Hungry children do not score as high as well-fed children.

Cultural Factors. This broad category covers a number of influences. In the Third International Mathematics and Science Study (TIMSS), most of the 41 countries participating, especially western countries, had eighth-grade test scores that were very similar. Five or six developing nations scored at the bottom, and four Asian nations — Singapore, Japan, Korea, and Hong Kong — scored high. (Taiwan did not take part; it would probably have been another high scorer.) In between were about 30 nations with few differences. In the high-scoring nations it is not unusual for students to go to school after school or to go to a private tutor. They also go to school on weekends. Here's a typical report from Japan:

> Akiko Tsutsui, a 10-year-old fifth-grader, gets out of school at 3:30 p.m. and goes straight home to have a snack and do her homework. Three afternoons a week she leaves again at 4:45 for a *juku* (cram school for tests) session that lasts from 5:10 to 10:00. For almost the entire class, Akiko will listen to tutors explain how to answer test questions and will practice taking them herself. (*Time,* 22 April 1996, p. 60)

And this from Korea:

> It was 11 p.m. and fourth-grader Moon Sae Bom was solving math problems and double-checking her social studies maps. For the past two hours, her mother had sat beside her, checking her answers, making sure the 10-year-old didn't fall asleep.

> Across this academically hyperachieving county, students file out of public and private high schools not at 3 p.m. but at 10 p.m. Every weeknight they study in their classrooms from dinner until late into the evening. (*Washington Post,* 7 May 1996, p. 1)

In Japan, it is critically important for the future that children get into the "right" high school and even more important later to get into the "right" college.

In Korea, the highest-scoring students will gain admission to one of the top three universities. These universities receive 285,000 applications and admit 1.5% of the applicants.

Under such conditions, it is not surprising to find students in these countries outscoring European and American students. The American vision of high school life includes malls, dating, cars, jobs and extracurricular activities at school. American kids are expected to crank it up, brainwise, in college. And they do. In contrast, Japanese students work extremely hard in high school, but stories abound of how they go into intellectual hibernation once they reach college. Their lives have been pretty much determined by getting into an institution of higher education. They might very well already know what company they will work for the rest of their lives when they graduate.

We observe in passing that, while Americans have been wondering how to get students' test scores up in international comparisons, high education officials from Asian nations have been visiting America to see how they can make their students more like ours. A June 9, 1997 editorial in *The Daily Yomiuri* declared that the Japanese school system was "obsolete and useless for the development of society." According to the editorial, the system doesn't develop artistic or cultural sensibility, doesn't promote an international perspective or social awareness, and "is ineffective in developing students' ability to think for themselves."

In 1997, the minister of education of Singapore, the highest-scoring nation in TIMSS, toured the United States. A reporter asked why he was here, given that his students had the highest test scores in the world. He expressed disdain that the only thing the students could do was answer test questions. When Korea revamped its mathematics curriculum, it relied principally on an American document: the standards, derided by some as "fuzzy math," produced by the National Council of Teachers of Mathematics.

CHAPTER 4

Standardized Tests

Achievement Tests, all commercial standardized achievement tests used in grades K-12.

What is standardized about standardized tests? The short answer is almost everything. The format of all questions for all students is the same — standardized. This format is usually, but not always, the multiple-choice format. The questions themselves for all students are the same — standardized. (Well into the 20th century, examinations were often oral, with each student getting different questions. And in some tests administered by computer, this is still true. These tests, known as computerized adaptive tests present some different items to different students depending on how well they have answered previous items.) The instructions to all students are the same — standardized. The time permitted for all students to complete the test is the same — standardized. (Students receiving certain special education services might be accorded more time to finish along with other adaptations such as large print, etc.) Standardized tests are often contrasted with "teacher-made" tests, but even these share many of the standardized characteristics listed above.

Standardized tests are most often administered to groups of students, but some, such as IQ tests, can be — or must be — given to individuals. In such cases, those who administer the tests have themselves been highly "standardized." That is, while they have some flexibility in the sequencing of questions and in applying the criteria for a correct answer, they must undergo extensive training to

Most of the tests that people take or are likely to read about in the newspapers are referred to as "standardized tests." The SAT is probably the best known of such tests, but anyone who has gone through school is likely to have encountered the Iowa Tests of Basic Skills (ITBS), the Iowa Tests of Educational Development, the Tests of Achievement and Proficiency, the Stanford Achievement Tests, the Comprehensive Tests of Basic Skills, or the Metropolitan become standardized in the way the tests are given and scored. A child should not get an IQ of 100 from one test administrator and 130 from another.

The methods used to construct standardized tests are themselves quite standardized, especially the methods for constructing the most commonly used tests: commercially published achievement tests used by schools. To construct these tests, test publishers cull the most common textbooks and curriculum materials and try to develop questions that reflect these materials. Curriculum specialists rate the items for what is termed "content validity," which simply is a rating by the experts as to whether or not they think the test actually measures what it claims to.

The questions are then tried out on groups of people to see if the questions "behave properly." Proper behavior in a test question is defined in statistical properties. These statistical procedures determine which items will be incorporated into the final version of a test.

In recent years, various states have wanted their "own" tests built to measure state-developed standards for students. The definition of content validity in these situations takes on an additional meaning. In order for a test item to have content validity, it must faithfully reflect the standard that it is supposed to measure.

About the only thing in a standardized testing setting that is not standardized is the test-taker. This lack of standardization among test-takers is something most often overlooked by test makers and test users — except in the case of very young children where the lack of standardization is so obvious it cannot be ignored.

The lack of work in this area could be an important omission. A recent study, for example, found that, even when everyone has enough time to finish a test, different students have different, but consistent, test-taking tempos. Some people will work faster than others, and this is a fairly consistent personality trait. One would expect that, when people with different tempos are put in settings where time *is* a factor — as in most test-taking situations — some people's performance will be badly distorted by time pressure.

Standardized test construction techniques can limit educational innovation. A test publisher naturally wants to sell a test to the widest possible market in order to obtain the largest possible profit. To have wide appeal, the test must reflect that which is common among schools, not that which is unique. If schools, teachers, or pupils are evaluated on the basis of test scores, education reformers will be loath to make innovations that might not be reflected in these scores.

Consider in this regard, the Key School, a magnet school in the Indianapolis Public School System. The teachers who founded the Key School were intrigued by the theory of multiple intelligences developed by psychologist Howard Gardner of Harvard University. In his 1983 book, *Frames of Mind,* Gardner outlined evidence for seven intelligences: linguistic, logical-mathematical, spatial, musical, bodily-kinesthetic, intrapersonal, and interpersonal. He has since added two more, naturalist and existential.

Gardner has chastised traditional schools for emphasizing only linguistic and logical-mathematical intelligences. The founders of the Key school wanted to develop all seven. Thus all children learn to play a musical instrument and receive daily lessons in art. Movement is emphasized during physical education. Teachers also teach "pods" — short courses about things that interest them. This is not a Gardner-oriented practice, but something based on the notion that teachers who teach about the things that turn them on outside of class might turn the kids on, too. Visitors to the Key School are usually impressed. It is obvious that the kids love being there. (The Key School began as a pre-kindergarten through grade 6 school; it expanded to the middle grades and high school grades in large part because its early graduates pleaded for such a school for their upper grades.)

Now many people would hold that it's a good thing to learn about art or to play a musical instrument or to speak, read, and write a foreign language. But acquiring these skills will do nothing to improve students' performance on any standardized achievement test. The vocabularies of art and music are too specialized to be a part of the reading or vocabulary sections of the ITBS. Specialized words in the lower grades do not lend themselves to the kind of items that have the statistical properties test makers are looking for (more about just what they're looking for later). Similarly, learning Spanish, the language chosen at the Key School, might one day help a student to see the Latin root of an otherwise mysterious word on the SAT, but it will not do anything for scores on the ITBS or any other K-12 achievement test.

A principle emerges from the above exposition: *tests should be used to evaluate schools (or anything else) only when it is clear that the test reflects what is being taught.* And it is the case that the test should reflect what is being taught, not that what is being taught should necessarily reflect the test. A second principle also emerges: *those who would reform the schools should seek instruments that they might reasonably expect to be sensitive to the effects of the changes they make.*

If it looks like the reform ought to push test scores upwards, then a test is a reasonable device to use to look for the reform's impact. But when, as with the Key School, the changes don't seem to have much relationship to test scores, then other instruments should be sought, or tests sensitive to the reforms should be developed. Unfortunately, at present, the only goal of most reformers is higher test scores.

As we saw earlier, the Russian launch of Sputnik in 1957 lead to massive curriculum reform in this country. Reformers developed new curricula and pedagogy for mathematics, physics, biology, and so on. Naturally, the question arose, Are these new curricula any better than the old ones? When students using various curricula were tested, the answer that emerged was: it depends. If the new curricula matched the tests, they looked good. If the tests matched the old curricula, the old curricula looked superior.

STANDARDIZED TESTS AND HOW PEOPLE LEARN

Robert Mislevy, in his 1993 article *Foundations of a New Test Theory,* wrote:

> It is only a slight exaggeration to describe the test theory that dominates educational measurement today as the application of 20th century statistics to 19th century psychology.[9]

Actually, Mislevy might have been too generous. Many tests don't consider psychology at all. When they do, according to the Committee on the Foundations of Assessment in *Knowing What Students Know,* "Current assessments are derived from early theories that characterize learning as a step-by-step accumulation of facts, procedures, definitions, and other discrete bits of knowledge and skills."[10]

Indeed, virtually all of today's tests ignore everything that has been learned by psychologists and cognitive scientists since the dawn of the 20th century. I know of only one test that does take account of such learning: the Wisconsin Reading Test, administered in third grade. That test at least attempts to get a fix on what the students know about the topics in the reading passages before they read a passage and also attempts to determine what kinds of reading strategies students employ. Nearly all tests emphasize that there is one right answer and penalize students who might not know the answer but know about the topic and can reason from it.

Consider two assessments adapted from *Knowing What Students Know* (p. 28):

Assessment 1

Question: What was the date of the battle of the Spanish Armada?
Answer: 1588 (correct).

Question: What can you tell me about what this meant?

Answer: Not much. It was one of the dates I memorized for the exam.

Assessment 2

Question: What was the date of the battle of the Spanish Armada?

Answer: It must have been around 1590.

Question: Why do you say that?

Answer: I know the English began to settle in Virginia just after 1600, not sure of the exact date. They wouldn't have dared start overseas settlements if Spain still had control of the seas. It would take a little while to get expeditions organized, so England must have gained naval supremacy somewhere in the late 1500s.

Many people would say that the student in the second assessment has better knowledge of the history involved, sees the implications of the battle in question, and can reason from what he knows to what the assessor asked. Most tests, though, would favor the student in assessment 1.

Today's tests also do not provide any information on how a student has organized his knowledge or on progress toward mastery of a skill. They rank students, or they evaluate a student in relation to some standard. The evaluation, though, tends to be vague: the student meets the criterion, performs poorly, etc. Tests offer the teacher no clue about what to do next.

Studies of experts and novices (for example, chess masters and beginners, physicists and students in a physics course) find that experts organize their knowledge differently from novices. It is possible that one day cognitive science will have described the steps along the way from beginner to expert such that a true set of criterion-referenced tests can be constructed (the nature of criterion-referenced tests is described in a later section).

In recent decades, researchers studying how people think have concluded that how people think about

> The test should reflect what is being taught, not that what is being taught should necessarily reflect the test.

their thinking is important. Thinking about thinking is usually called "metacognition," "meta" being a Greek word for "over." When we think, when we try to solve a problem, or when we engage in any cognitive activity, we monitor our thinking even as we think. Tests don't test this.

If all you want to do is spread people out in order to make predictions about how they'll fare at some later task — the original purpose of testing — then you can probably ignore developments in our knowledge of how people learn. But the avowed goal of testing today is to improve education and student achievement. For that, you need something other than today's tests.

The Committee on the Foundations of Assessment presents a vision for testing in the future.[11] The view presented looks Utopian, to me. Sorry to sound pessimistic, but I can't imagine this vision taking hold, given the political status of testing and the greed of the test publishers.

Norm-Referenced Tests

A norm-referenced test is a standardized test with a norm. The norm, in turn, is a rank — the 50th percentile — that is assigned to the "median" score, the median being one kind of average.[12] It is also the score that test makers call "at grade level." By definition, then, half of all test-takers score at or above the 50th percentile, and half score below it. Half score above grade level, and half score below it.

It bothers some people that a norm-referenced test, by definition, labels half of our children as below average. The nature of a norm or grade level also leads to confusion. Some people, politicians usually, can be heard decrying the fact that even a small percentage of a given group of students scored below grade level. The cries happen most frequently when the phrase "grade level" is used because people naturally think that everyone in, say, the seventh grade, should be at or above seventh-grade level. People who utter such cries don't realize that the way tests are constructed guarantees that, nationally, half of all children are below grade level.

If a norm is to be meaningful at the national level, it has to be something more then the 50th percentile of the South Succotash School System. To determine the norm, test publishers first try out their questions on students and choose the questions that behave properly. By and large, this means choosing questions that about 50% of the students miss. Some questions will be easier, and some will be harder. But rarely do tests include questions that 90% of the students get right or that 90% get wrong.

Why is 50% such a magical number? It isn't magical; it is an artifact of the history of testing in this country. As discussed previously, early testers wanted to predict who would make good tank drivers or, good artillery men. After the war, they wanted to predict who would make good college students.

Well, if you want to make differential predictions, you have to arrange it so that different people get different scores. For instance, if you want to use height to predict who will be good at basketball and everyone who shows up is 6' 6" tall, then you can't use height, because everyone has the same "score." You need some players who are 6' 3", some who are 7' 2", and some who are in between these extremes so you can determine whether the tall guys play better than the shorties.

Similarly, if you choose items that everyone misses or everyone gets right, then everyone gets the same test score, and you can't make differential predictions. Fine, you say. You're not interested in such predictions. But that is all that the early test developers *were* interested in.

It turns out that, if you choose items that, on average, 50% of the test-takers get right and 50% get wrong, you end up with a test that distributes scores in a normal, bell-shaped curve and maximizes the dispersion of the scores (trust me on this or check a textbook on testing for it's a bit too technical to get into here).

Test developers will also reject items that people with low total scores get right or that people with high total scores get wrong. They think that there must be something peculiar about any particular item that the high scorers have trouble with or that the low scorers find a snap. Maybe there's something peculiar about one of the distractors (the testing industry's name for the wrong answers presented in multiple-choice questions) that's causing the high scorers to make a mistake. Who knows? In any case, the item is dumped.

The very presence of "distractors" bothers a number of test critics. The test publishers must trick some students into choosing a wrong answer. If they cannot do that, then the item will not "behave" properly. That is, it will not be missed by half of the students. A system based on such deliberate deception bothers people.

The above considerations tell us something important about test construction: in the end, much of what determines whether a question will be on a test has nothing to do with the content of the test. Whether a question gets on a test has to do with technical, statistical concerns about how the item "behaves." As Oscar Buros, author of *The Mental Measurements Yearbook,* once observed, a technician could look at the statistical properties of test items and construct an entire test that would "behave" properly — spread out the scores of test-takers — without ever actually looking at any of the items.

Once the test publisher has a set of well-behaved items, the company conducts what is called a national norming study. That is, it administers the test to a large group of children, maybe as many as 200,000 in all grades. These children have been selected so that they are representative of the nation. That is, the group has the same mix of black, white, Hispanic, Asian, Native American, rich, middle-class, poor, urban, suburban, and rural students as the nation as a whole. The median score of this group, the 50th percentile, is then called the "national norm." While it may be possible for "all the children" in Lake Wobegon or any other small locality to be "above average," even Garrison Keillor can't make that true for the entire nation. Again, by definition, half of the students in the nation will always be below average.

A norm-referenced test gives scores in relation to the norm, the 50th percentile, hence its name. If your child brings home a report that says he scored at the 75th percentile, you know that he scored better than 75% of the students in the national norming sample and that 25% of those students scored better than your child. (We will discuss percentiles and other technical terms used in reporting test results in a later section.) You do not know from a percentile whether your child is doing well or poorly or average in any other sense.

What if a community scores well on a norm-referenced test? It could mean that the students are smart or that their school system is good or both. It could also mean that they're just rich. Wealthy communities spend more on their schools, and affluent families are able to provide resources at home that low-income families cannot. Communities that are below the norm in wealth sometimes complain that it is unfair to compare them to a national norm that includes wealthy communities as well as poor ones.

As a consequence, in addition to the national norm, test companies develop a variety of "local" norms: low-income communities can compare themselves to other low-income communities, suburban communities can compare themselves to other suburbs, private schools can compare themselves to other private schools. But suburbs seldom compare themselves to other suburbs because they look better compared to national norms. On the other hand, a low-income community will probably look better compared to other low-income communities than to the nation.

This illustrates a problem with "local norms" in education: they can obscure real problems. An inner-city school system using local norms for urban districts can say, "We're doing as well as expected, and we'd be doing just as well as the rest of the country if we didn't have all these poor kids to educate." But that system *does* have all those poor kids to educate. And, as we saw earlier, poverty depresses test scores.

It is important to emphasize that percentile ranks — any ranks — obscure actual performance. From ranks alone you can tell nothing about the performance. When they run the final heat of the hundred-meter dash in the Olympics, someone finishes last. Someone *must* rank last. That runner is still the eighth-fastest human being on the planet that day and probably is not referred to by his friends as "Pokey."

Domains vs. Tests. We should note an important aspect of all tests — norm-referenced and others — that often gets overlooked in discussions of testing. We speak of tests of reading, mathematics, history, and so forth as if they were generic tests of reading, mathematics, history, and so forth. But they are not. They are short tests of specific skills, often tested in peculiar ways. The multiple-choice format is but a proxy for actual performance, and sometimes it is not a good proxy.

Achievement test publishers admit that their tests can't cover everything. How could they? They're

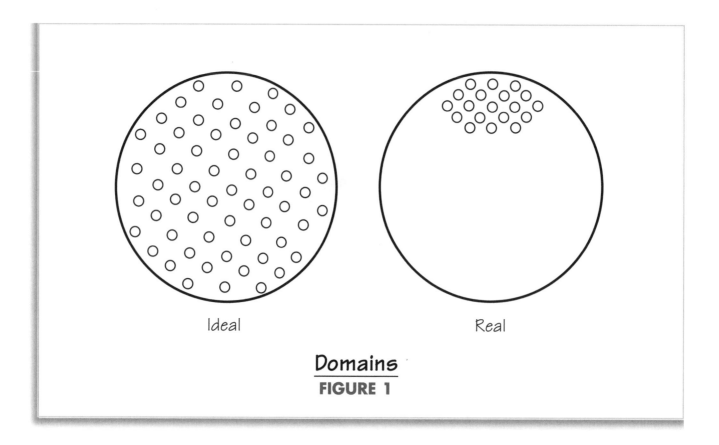

Ideal   Real

Domains
FIGURE 1

only 25 to 40 items long. The publishers will contend that their tests sample a larger "domain." The notion of domain sampling is represented by the left circle in Figure 1. The big circle represents a domain such as mathematics. The little circles represent what the items on the test are supposed to do: they sample small parts of the entire domain. This is in contrast to the right circle in Figure 1. There, the items sample more intensely a small part of the overall domain. This comes closer to representing what criterion-referenced tests are supposed to do. Note, though, the blank areas of the right circle: large parts of the domain are entirely omitted. This happens when teaching becomes concentrated on aspects of the curriculum covered by a particular tests.

For either type of test, the theory of domain sampling is largely nonsense because no one has ever specified what a curriculum "domain" is. All the tests really do is ask specific questions in specific ways.

We can see the specific skills aspect of tests clearly by looking at old mathematics tests. In the 1960s some mathematicians had decided that the understanding of mathematics was best conveyed through set theory. As a consequence, students even in elementary grades were learning such terms as "null set, associativity, and commutativity" — words that most of their teachers did not understand (and, for the record, neither does the spell-checker on my computer). The mathematics tests of the period contained many questions using the terminology and concepts of set theory. If children today were to take these tests, they would score abysmally low because the words would mystify them. It would look like today's kids don't know "mathematics" at all. But what they really don't know is a particular approach to mathematics and the language it uses.

Similarly, an elementary reading test predicated on word-attack skills would look very different from one predicated on whole language and comprehension. And the same child would do well or not so well depending on what kind of instruction he or she had received. There really is no such thing as a "domain" of reading or mathematics that a test samples. Domains are just convenient fictions for test publishers.

Multiple-Choice Format. The multiple-choice format is a peculiar way of measuring something. We have already noted that the test publisher must successfully trick students into choosing wrong answers if the items are to "behave" properly. Beyond this problem, there is the question of what is being measured.

We can see this problem most readily in connection with writing. For a number of years, when multiple-choice tests were virtually the only form used, "writing" was assessed with items that really measure only editing skills. For instance, students would look at a sentence and decide what was wrong with it by choosing one of the four or five choices of "corrections" provided. Or the test might show a short paragraph with four or five parts of it underlined. The student's task was to decide which underlined section contained an error (or if none of them did). Since they were being evaluated on their students' performance on tests of this type of editing skill, teachers naturally taught this type of editing skill. As a consequence, children did not learn to write.

When educators later came to their senses and realized that students must actually write in order to learn how to write, children's writing improved. However, having students actually write something collides with the need to keep scoring costs low. So in many large-scale assessments, children are now taught formulas, not real writing. Teachers report they can now ask students, "How many sentences are there in a paragraph?" and get an answer.

The real answer, of course, is "It depends on what you're writing about." But the kids know The Answer is five. The students are taught that paragraphs must contain an opening topic sentence, three supporting sentences, and a closing sentence.

The teachers have learned that that's the way the test company's temporary workers — paid at just above minimum wage — will score them. Any student who shows any creativity in their brief essays will get a low grade.

Another odd aspect of multiple-choice tests was captured wonderfully by one T. C. Batty in a 1959 letter to the *Times* of London:

Sir,

Among the "odd one out" type of questions which my son had to answer for a school entrance examination was, "Which is the odd one out among cricket, football, billiards, and hockey?"

I say billiards because it is the only one played indoors. A colleague says football because it is the only one in which the ball is not struck with an implement. A neighbor says cricket because in all the other games the object is to put the ball into a net; and my son, with the confidence of nine summers, plumps for hockey "because it is the only one that is a girls' game." Could any of your readers put me out of my misery by stating what is the correct answer, and further enlighten me by explaining how questions of this sort prove anything, **especially when the scholar has merely to underline the odd one out without giving a reason?**

Perhaps there is a remarkable subtlety behind all this. Is the question designed to test what a child of 9 may or may not know about billiards — proficiency at which may still be regarded as the sign of a misspent youth?

Yours faithfully,
T. C. Batty

There is not, unfortunately, any kind of "remarkable subtlety" behind such a question. Readers did not put Batty out of his misery, although they did write many letters offering still more reasons why one particular game was the odd one out. It was doubtless great fun for *Times* readers, though we might well wonder how much fun the experience was for Batty's son and his classmates. The test, after all, evaluated them on their qualifications for admission to elite schools, at the ripe old age of 9.

I have put in italics the part of the letter that reveals an unavoidable problem with multiple-choice tests: you have no idea why students might have picked a particular answer. Did they guess? Did they recall it by rote? Did they reason their way to a right answer? Did they reason their way to a wrong answer? Does their knowledge extend to a "deep" level or do they know the topic at some surface level that allows them to pick the right answer but not to use the concept in any way?

Young children especially can often give quite plausible reasons for choosing a "wrong" answer — if asked. In one situation, for instance, children were asked, "What animal is most likely to be found on a farm: elephant, giraffe, chicken, fox?" Most children picked giraffe. They chose giraffe because a nearby petting zoo was named "Animal Farm" and used a wooden giraffe to mark the entrance. Unfortunately, in the usual testing situation, no one asks children to explain their choices.

What You Test Is What You Get. One final condition of testing that deserves comment here is the Law of WYTIWYG (pronounced wittywig): What You Test Is What You Get. There are two aspects of this law. The first and most obvious is that teachers will spend more time on the topics the test covers than they will on topics not covered by the test. This is especially true if the test is a high-stakes test (see pages 21-23 for a discussion of high-stakes testing). But even if the only sanctions are the emphases given test scores by the school staff, the school board, the media, or local industry, the law still holds. Thus it is very important to use tests that reflect instructional priorities and that do

not in and of themselves cause the curriculum to become narrowed by teaching to the test.

Teaching to most school tests is a problem because it constitutes "cheating." But that is not the real problem. A high school football coach teaches to the test all week long, and we don't call it cheating. Indeed, we would think him crazy if he did anything else. But in this instance, the "test" is a real-life experience to prepare for. Many achievement tests, though, are in no way "real-life" experiences. A teacher can teach to a test, but it comes at the expense of not teaching other parts of the curriculum.

More important, real life does not come to us in a multiple-choice format. That is the real problem of teaching to most tests, and that is one reason there has been such an increased interest in "performance tests" — tests that measure actual performance rather than tests where students are provided the answers in multiple-choice format — since the mid 1980s.

There is, however, a second and more subtle aspect of testing related to the Law of WYTIWYG: how you test determines, in part, what you see. When you measure people using a multiple-choice test, some people will do well, and others won't. When you measure people using a performance assessment, some people will do well, and others won't. But they won't always be the same people. In educational testing, how you measure something determines, in part, what you see.

Moreover, in the best of all testing worlds, people are indeed altered by the measurement: the best testing informs as well as assesses. Athletes often return from their "tests," saying "I learned something out there today." Students seldom walk away from a testing situation with the same sense of accomplishment. It's possible, though.

CRITERION-REFERENCED TESTS
How a person stands relative to the norm or to other people — a normative score — is not the only possible kind of score. However, normative

scores are overwhelmingly the easiest to obtain and, as a consequence, are the most common. It is possible, however, to score performance in relation to "a clearly specified set of behaviors," not in relation to other people. The tests that score in relationship to behaviors are known as criterion-referenced tests (CRTs). Most of these tests were not really criterion-referenced, but that gets us ahead of our story.

What is a "clearly specified set of behaviors?" As I noted earlier, we have a hard time specifying such behaviors for the topics taught in school. So most examples of clearly specified behaviors were taken from other areas. The inventor of the phrase "criterion-referenced testing," Robert Glaser of the University of Pittsburgh, said that we could imagine achievement as a continuum of specified behaviors from zero performance to conspicuous excellence and place any given performance somewhere along that continuum.[13] For example, if ice skating was chosen as the clearly specified set of behaviors, then we could imagine a zero point as "Can't stand alone on ice." Conspicuous excellence at the other end of the continuum might be "Completes triple axel with perfect landing." A triple axel is a specific set of behaviors that judges can rate with near perfect agreement. In between zero and the triple axel are many intermediate levels of accomplishment. The standards for these accomplishments (the criteria of CRT) can also be described, and the performance of the skater evaluated in reference to them.

The world of education is somewhat vaguer and more complex, but Glaser's idea generated a great deal of enthusiasm. The notion of CRTs, in the words of the late psychometrician Jason Millman "totally destroyed the monopoly of norm-referenced interpretations that was held in many quarters." In 1994, Millman reflected on how he and many others initially reacted to the concept of a CRT:

> Thirty years ago I was a young pup, full of ambition and optimism. I thought that if only educators could write good test specifications, explicitly stating what was and was not part of

the content coverage, CRTs would be able to meet their promise. More than that, even, I believed CRTs could give quantitative interpretations such as: Billy can answer 65% of the questions contained in a given domain. But I was wrong.[14]

Many other psychometricians experienced Millman's enthusiasm and subsequent disillusionment. What happened? Basically, the testers found that they couldn't specify educational outcomes with the same clarity that they could specify the outcomes of ice skating. Ice skating is easy to observe, but what's in a kid's head is not. It is also difficult to infer from a test precisely what the student knows. More important, ice skating is a very limited range of behaviors. The goals of education are more general.

Although criterion-referenced tests became all the rage in the 1970s, they were a problem: they had no criteria. Or, more precisely, a "criterion" was imposed on a test through the act of setting a "cut score" for passing or failing. Thus the "criterion" on tests was a certain score, called the cut score. Above this score, you pass. Below it, you fail. This is hardly the kind of criterion Glaser had in mind. It reduced criterion-referenced tests to nothing more than norm-referenced tests without the norms.

The use of cut scores has itself been controversial and problematic, particularly in the use of "minimum competency" or other high-stakes tests to determine grade promotion or eligibility for graduation. Such tests were tests said to consist of "minimal" or "essential" skills. This gave people the impression that all test-takers should attain perfect scores, otherwise they would fail in life. So what did it mean, then, to set a cut score at, say, 60% correct, a commonly used figure?

More troublesome was the concept of minimum competency. Should a student who scored 61% be permitted to graduate while a student who scored 59% was forced to repeat his entire senior year or receive something less than a diploma?

Such decisions are particularly troubling in view of the existence of something the test makers call "measurement error" (discussed in the section on technical concerns). No test is perfectly accurate. If you gave a student a test, then somehow obliterated his memory of it and gave it to him again the next day, it is most unlikely that his score would be exactly the same.

The measurement error of a test can be estimated statistically, and for a number of tests used for promotion-retention decisions or graduation eligibility, it is quite large. Good practice would require that this error at least be taken into account in setting a cut score, but real practice has seldom emulated good practice, in part because these tests emerged largely from political concerns rather than educational concerns.

The kinds of issues concerning cut scores were never really resolved — they are, in fact, not resolvable by technical means although taking measurement error into account is technically useful. Cut scores these days reflect more political desires than anything else. We noted the capricious way the Virginia State Board of Education set cut scores, and we mentioned California's even more careless approach.

In the years since the initial popularity of CRTs and minimum competency programs, the sanctions for not passing the tests have stiffened. In Maryland, for instance, students who do not pass the state tests (now set for 2006-2007) get nothing. Virginia has a similar program. In North Carolina, students who do not score above a certain level on that state's tests are denied diplomas, and the state has recently instituted a retention-by-test-score policy. Students with unsatisfactory scores are given the test again. If they fail again, they go to summer school and take the test again. If they fail again, they repeat the grade.

Before leaving this section, we should observe that the difference between an NRT and a CRT is one of usage and interpretation, not of form. The distinction is not a necessary distinction. The SAT might be viewed as a sorta-kinda blend. It has norms — the average student scores 500. It also has a criterion, freshman grade-point average, although that is not the kind of "clearly specified behaviors" the early workers in the field had in mind.

Seldom does one test serve both purposes well, but it would be possible to collect norms for a CRT, and it is possible, albeit very difficult, to give a criterion-referenced interpretation to NRTs. In fact, the city of Chicago has done this, although it appears that a new superintendent appointed in 2001 has abandoned the practice. Formerly, students with low scores on the ITBS were simply retained. This is a wholly inappropriate use of the ITBS.

PERFORMANCE TESTS

Beginning in the late 1980s, some people in the assessment field did more than just express frustrations over the limits of multiple-choice tests. They began experimenting with tests that actually required students to perform. These tests became popularly known as "authentic tests" although some objected to this name because it implied that other forms of testing were "inauthentic" or phony. The term authentic was used because the tasks they required of students were authentic problems from the real world, not artificial situations in which a student had to read a short "stem" and then select one of the alternatives provided by the test maker. These new tests were a type of performance test, and performance test is probably a better generic term than authentic test so we'll go with that.

When Jason Millman referred to the monopoly of NRTs, all of them were multiple-choice tests (a few have since added some small performance measures, notably writing and, to a lesser extent, mathematics questions where the students must solve the problem and explain their reasoning). Performance testing had virtually disappeared from schools although it remained a valued type of testing in other arenas, notably the military, performing and fine arts, and vocational education. Those in military service were often required to perform in a simulation of something they would later face in the field. Musicians have always performed in recitals and competitions. Actors auditioned and rehearsed. Artists and architects were "tested" through displays of their works: portfolios. Students in vocational education built cabinets, repaired engines, etc.

In schools, performance assessments occurred in some vocational areas and in sports — what is practice on the football field besides getting ready for the "test" on Friday night? But, save for writing, they were seldom seen in the academic areas. As noted earlier, after years of using multiple-choice editing tasks, educators realized that writing could not be adequately tested in the absence of having the students write something.

Some assessment professionals wanted to bring performance tests into the schools. Analogies seemed compelling. After all, when we fly, we are not especially interested in whether the pilot can fill in an answer sheet about the instruments in the cockpit. We want to know if he can get the plane up in the air, across to our destination, and down on the ground again safely.

Performance tests, for the most part, are not "standardized" in the ways that the tests we discussed earlier are "standardized." When all students respond to the same writing "prompt" in a writing assessment, then some amount of standardization is involved, especially if they must all finish in a given amount of time and are given no opportunity to edit and revise. But performance tests introduce a degree of idiosyncrasy into the assessment situation.

As an aside, a number of people prefer to use the word "assessment" when referring to a performance test. The English word "assessment" comes from an old French word and is related to the modern French verb *s'assoir*, to sit oneself down. The idea is that, while a test might be done by "remote control," an assessment requires the assessor to sit down beside the student, much as a doctor might sit down next to a patient. It is only in this more intimate and intense context that the

> Why are performance tests so seldom seen in schools? Performance tests take a lot of time and so cost a lot of money.

assessor can really assess the student. In the following discussion, I use "test" and "assessment" interchangeably.

Why are performance tests so seldom seen in schools? There are several reasons. In all the examples of performance testing listed, only small numbers of people are involved at any one time. Performance tests take a lot of time and so cost a lot of money. If the goal of an assessment can be reached by using the much faster, much cheaper multiple-choice tests, then there is little reason to spend the extra time, effort, and money on performance assessments. And recall that, in the history of testing in this country, the emphasis has been on making discriminations among people, not on determining how well they actually perform. Paper-and-pencil tests can spread people out in a bell curve much faster and cheaper than performance measures. Similarly, if the interest is in obtaining some idea of how well a school or, more likely, a school system is functioning, the use of performance assessments would be horrendously expensive and time-consuming.

However, there are many aspects of education (and life) that do not lend themselves well to multiple-choice tests. The most obvious school-related area has already been mentioned, writing. One cannot measure writing skills by means of multiple-choice questions. More important, children cannot learn to write by practicing the editing skills that can be assessed through multiple-choice tests. Children must write to learn how to write. This statement seems so obvious that one wonders why it was ignored for so long.

The statement "children must write to learn how to write" illustrates another aspect of good testing: good testing does not simply measure performance, it informs it. People can learn something from it. Not much can be learned from taking a multiple-choice test. Compare the following questions:

What is the volume of a cone that has a base area of 78 square centimeters and a height of 12 centimeters?

a. 30 cm3   c. 936 cm3
b. 312 cm3   d. 2,808 cm3

This is a fairly typical multiple-choice item that might occur on a geometry test. A series of such items would provide some idea of how well students know the formulas for calculating volumes of different shapes, although it would provide no information about *why* students had chosen the answer they picked. It is also a decontextualized question. That is, it has no real-life context, no way for the student to know why the volume of a cone might be important. The student gains nothing from providing a correct answer to this question.

In contrast, consider this performance task:

Background. Manufacturers naturally want to spend as little as possible not only on the product, but on packaging it and shipping it to stores. They want to *minimize* the cost of their packaging, and they want to *maximize* the amount of what is packaged inside (to keep handling and postage costs down: the more individual packages you ship, the more it costs).

Setting. Imagine that your group of two or three people is one of many in the packaging department responsible for packing M & M's candies for shipment. The manager of the shipping department has found that the cheapest material for shipping comes as a flat piece of rectangular paperboard (the piece of posterboard you will be given). She is asking each group in the packaging department to help solve this problem: *What completely closed container, built out of the given piece of posterboard, will hold the largest volume of M & M's candies for safe shipping?*

1. *Prove,* in a convincing written report to company executives, that both the shape and the dimensions of your group's container maximize the volume. In making your case, supply all important data and formulas. Your group will also be asked to make a three-minute oral report at the next staff meeting. Both reports will be judged for *accuracy, thoroughness, and persuasiveness.*

2. Build a *model* (or multiple models) of your proposed container out of the posterboard. The models are not *proof;* they *illustrate* the claims that you offer in your report.

Here we have a real-life, challenging problem, borrowed, incidentally, from Grant Wiggins' *Assessing Student Performance.* Students must be able to justify their answers. They must work with others. They actually have to structure part of the problem themselves. Knowing formulas is necessary, but not sufficient.

This problem meets the criteria of the "new basics," as described by economists Richard Murnane of Harvard and Frank Levy of MIT in their 1996 book, *Teaching the New Basics.* Murnane and Levy analyzed the job requirements for jobs that would pay at least a middle-class wage. They list six skills, only two of which are actually new in terms of what people have proposed that schools should teach. One is "the ability to solve semi-structured problems where hypotheses must be formed and tested." The other is "the ability to work in groups with persons of various backgrounds." I would add to these two new skills "the ability to communicate effectively, both orally and in writing."

The employers whose job requirements Murnane and Levy studied told them that too many of our high school graduates lacked these skills. Of course, there is a little self-interest in the employers saying this: they might be able to get the schools to do for free what they now have to pay for in on-the-job training. In addition, since almost two-thirds of high school graduates enter some form of higher education the next fall, the most academically capable students are not showing up to apply for jobs straight out of high school. International comparisons indicate that American students' performance in reading is excellent (in relation to other countries) and adequate in math and science. Some of the skills Murnane and Levy say American high school graduates don't have appeared to be quite well-developed in eighth-graders and even in some instances in fourth-graders.

However, the three new skills listed look important beyond the narrow confines of the workplace. For instance, when you buy a car (or a house), you have to structure the problem in terms of how many passengers you need room for, how much money you can afford to spend, how much fun you want to get from driving the car, what kind of mileage you want to get from it, and a host of other factors. One of the biggest aids in solving a problem, most any problem, is to be able to accurately frame the problem.

Moreover, thinking about a problem like what car to buy involves another kind of thinking: learning to evaluate tradeoffs. Multiple-choice problems are rare in real life. The choices in life are usually complex and involve tradeoffs. Do I want the friendly confines of a small liberal arts college, or am I more content in the anonymity of a large research university? I can probably get more personal attention at a small school, but I can take more specialized courses at a big one. Am I more likely to find someone I want to marry at a small school or a big one? The list could go on.

This is important. Schooling should be, in part, about teaching people to think. The ability to critically evaluate information is crucial to functioning in a democratic society. In totalitarian societies, you will be told what to think and brave or foolish if you express views to the contrary.

Some have argued that multiple-choice tests can test higher-order thinking skills. It is true that such tests *can* test higher-order skills, but they rarely do. Usually, multiple-choice tests that require thinking are found in a limited range of courses in graduate school. For instance, in my graduate course in learning theory, the professor used multiple-choice questions. However, the stem of these questions would describe an entire experiment and maybe take up one and a half 8" by 14" sheets of paper. We then answered questions about the experiment: Was the methodology right? Were the statistics appropriate? Was the researchers' conclusion justified by the results? And so on.

Most tests *punish* the thinking test-taker. Thinking takes time. And as a test-taker, the last thing you want while taking most tests is something that slows you down the way thinking does. Even the College Board agrees. In one of its SAT-preparation booklets, one piece of advice to those taking the SAT is "keep moving."

We can see the import of thinking and the difficulty of using multiple-choice tests to assess thinking by describing higher-order thinking. Lauren Resnick, a cognitive psychologist at the University of Pittsburgh, has spent a lot of time studying higher-order thinking and has concluded that it's a lot like the classic definition of pornography: I can't define it, but I'll know it when I see it. Even so, in *Education and Learning to Think,* Resnick listed some of the qualities of higher-order thinking can be described in general:

HIGHER-ORDER THINKING

1. is nonalgorithmic. That is, the path of action is not fully specified in advance [this is analogous to having to structure a problem].

2. tends to be complex. The total path is not "visible" (mentally speaking) for any single vantage point.

3. often yields multiple solutions, each with costs and benefits, rather than unique solutions.

4. involves nuanced judgment and interpretation.

5. involves the application of multiple criteria, which sometimes conflict with one another.

6. often involves uncertainty. Not everything that bears on the task at hand is known.

7. involves self-regulation of the thinking process. We do not recognize higher-order thinking in an individual when someone else "calls the plays" at every step.

8. involves imposing meaning, finding structure in apparent disorder.

9. is effortful. There is considerable mental work involved in the kinds of elaborations and judgments required.[15]

A student who deploys higher-order thinking, as defined above, while taking the SAT is in trouble. Time will expire before the student can finish. The reader might want to take these qualities of higher-order thinking and match them against the requirements of the M & M's problem described earlier.

Students solving the M & M's problem — taken from a real class in a real school — would also learn something in the process. The assessment would inform as well as measure.

Performance tests are not without their problems, aside from their costs in time and money. For instance, while the outcomes of the M & M's problem are fairly straightforward, there are ambiguities in the use of many other kinds of performance assessments. For example, portfolios are used in a number of places as the major portion of writing assessment. Decisions have to be made as to what goes into a portfolio. The student's best work or the student's typical work? The teacher's selection of "best work" or the student's? How many writing types will be required? Students with an aptitude for narration might want to concentrate on stories, ignoring essays, technical reports, and poetry. Who grades the portfolio? Different teachers judge the same work differently. While this has been considered largely in terms of teacher unreliability, it can also reflect genuine philosophical differences. One solution to this problem has been to train teachers to judge certain aspects of writing in similar ways. But does this cause them to overlook other meaningful qualities of the students' writing?

Or consider work done by groups. If the work is done in a group, but grades are to be assigned to individuals, the question arises as to whose work is it? Some parents object to group projects, alleging that a few kids end up doing all the work. Other parents accept this as good preparation for real life.

For reasons mentioned at the outset, multiple-choice tests will no doubt continue to flourish. For accountability and differentiation among students, it is hard to see how performance tests can replace them. Parents, though, it seems to me, should be concerned that performance tests at least become part of their children's educational experiences.

Given the educational climate of the day, I should say something about the issue of knowledge versus thinking skills. Educators have been looking primarily at the national move toward an Information Society and have emphasized thinking skills. E. D. Hirsch, Jr., foremost among another group, has contended that such an approach is anti-knowledge, while knowledge remains critical to our functioning as a coherent society.

Hirsch is wrong, I think, to argue that American schools don't teach knowledge. There are numerous analyses of textbooks and observations of American teachers that suggest just the opposite: the schools are too concerned with factual minutiae. We teach plenty of knowledge. I just think we don't teach it very coherently. Students might read, for no good reason, the same book in three elementary grades. Hirsch's "core curriculum" does provide some coherence and structure. On the other hand, numerous people have objected to the specific things included and excluded from that curriculum. Hirsch is right, in my opinion, that knowledge is critical. From all that I have read, learning stuff makes it easier to learn more stuff, virtually independent of what you learn. I think it is possible, too, that memorization actually can lead to understanding.

On the other hand, the Annenberg/CPB videotape series *Minds of Our Own* makes a compelling case for performance assessment. It opens with an interviewer handing a student a bulb, a wire, and a battery and asking if they can make the bulb light with this equipment. Some can and do. Some can't. And some say it can't be done. The last two results are disturbing since the students are in cap and gown, about to graduate from Harvard and MIT. The series goes on to show that, if teachers teach by lecturing and test with paper-and-pencil tests, they are virtually prevented from really knowing if the students have truly understood what the teachers were trying to impart.

APTITUDE, ABILITY, AND ACHIEVEMENT TESTS

Few notions in testing have caused more mischief than the distinctions between aptitude, ability, and achievement tests. Let's get it straight at the start: conceptually, the three are indistinguishable. Ability and aptitude tests do not measure something qualitatively different from what achievement tests measure.

The trouble begins when people assume, as they all-too-often do, that an aptitude or ability test measures "potential." Given a measure of potential, we can then see if children have "lived up to their potential." Accordingly, we can then label the children as "where they ought to be," "under-achievers," or "overachievers" according to whether their performance in school or on an achievement test matches their performance on the test of "potential." We could with just as much logic label a child an "overtester" or "undertester."

That there is no conceptual distinction between ability tests and achievement tests has been known for many years, but it is something that just doesn't enter into the everyday discussion of tests. But as long ago as 1960, in the second edition of his *Essentials of Psychological Testing*, the eminent psychometrician Lee Cronbach observed the essential nondistinction between the two kinds of tests:

> An aptitude test is one used to predict success in some occupation or training course. *In form, these tests are not distinctly different from other types.* The test is referred to as an achievement test when it is used to examine a person's success in past study, and as an aptitude test when it is used to forecast his success in some future course or assignment. (Emphasis added.)

For Cronbach, an achievement test looks back in time; an ability or aptitude test looks forward. But, in fact, this is a mere convention. We typically use the SAT to predict college success, and we use tests such as the Stanford Achievement Tests to gauge accomplishment in high school. But there is no reason why we couldn't use the Stanford to predict college success. (Using the SAT to summarize achievement would be somewhat less valid because the SAT tests only verbal and quantitative reasoning while an achievement test battery also includes science and social studies.) Such prediction is merely a statistical process, the calculation of a correlation coefficient (discussed in the section on technicalities). We take the scores from our test — SAT or Stanford or any other test — and correlate those scores with the freshmen grade-point averages of those we tested.

We could use high school grade-point averages to predict success in college — and they actually work better than the SAT at most universities. We could even use height or weight to predict college success, though the predictions might not be very useful. All we need to predict first-year college success are two variables: college freshman grade-point averages and *anything else* that varies: height, weight, SAT scores, finger length, etc. Remember, any two variables can be correlated. Whether or not the correlation is meaningful is another question. Predicting college grades from the SAT merely means correlating these two variables, a simple statistical procedure.

The real difference between ability and aptitude tests on the one hand and achievement tests on the other is that we have a better idea of why a student does well or not well on an achievement test. Even if an achievement test doesn't strictly reflect the curriculum — e.g., a phonics-based reading test given to a whole-language class — it still reflects to some extent what is being learned in school, reading. Ability tests often don't.

For example, the Cognitive Abilities Test (CogAT) includes a "non-verbal" section that requires students, among other things, to look at a series of geometrical forms and choose from an array of forms the one that would come next in the series. Some kids are really good at this, and some are awful. But it is unlikely that any of them received

instruction in "geometric form prediction" from their teachers or from their parents or from kids' TV. (By the way, the CogAT has two other sections, verbal and quantitative. Kids who do well on the nonverbal section and poorly on the verbal and quantitative have a terrible time coping with school — school is all about numbers and words. Kids who have this pattern of skills are often good at art, videogames, and perceptually oriented activities like chess.)

To repeat: in a single sitting, with a test given only once, you cannot measure potential. You can measure only what the student knows and can do at the time you test him. You can use that measure to look either forward or backward in time.

Perhaps a more meaningful assessment of ability could be obtained from multiple measures. If we tested a student in the fall and again in the spring and measured how much better she did in the spring than in the fall, we might use this difference as a measure of ability in terms of rate of learning, though it's still not a measure of "potential." Although this idea is plausible, no one has systematically tried to develop this concept of ability (a few people have dabbled at it).

It is unlikely that we will stop distinguishing between ability and achievement tests any time soon. The idea that there is such a distinction is deeply embedded in our culture and in our everyday language. In the sports world, for instance, it is common to hear commentators say that a certain athlete "has the most raw ability" of anyone on the team or that an athlete "never developed his ability fully." Similar statements are just as common in the academic realm. We just don't hear them on primetime TV.

INTERNATIONAL TESTS
"International Tests" are not a "type" of test. But the increasing popularity and prevalence of international comparisons require us to discuss them. The Third International Mathematics and Science Study (TIMSS) is the source of a new urban legend. As voiced by former secretary of education William

Bennett to the Heritage Foundation, it comes out this way: "In America today, the longer you stay in school, the dumber you get relative to kids from other industrialized nations." Below, I will actually accept part of this myth and dispatch another part.

The rationale for emphasizing international comparisons was folksily put once by Albert Shanker, then President of the American Federation of Teachers. I had presented a lot of data indicating increases in the scores of American kids on American tests. Al said, "I don't care if my 1992 car runs a little better than my 1972 car. What I care about is whether or not it runs better than those German and Japanese models parked across the street." In this view, progress on domestically administered tests doesn't matter so much as how we stack up against the rest of the world.

International comparisons have been conducted since the 1960s, but they garnered little attention outside of the education community because they suffered a variety of problems. Countries didn't pick representative samples, for instance. Most nations do not have a culture of public self-criticism as the United States does. Left to their own devices, many nations will choose to test those students who will make them look good.

This problem was compounded by greatly varying proportions of students in secondary schools in other countries. In the Second International Mathematics Study (SIMS), for instance, 100% of Hungarian students were still taking math courses in their final year of secondary school. But only 50% of that age group was still in school. It was difficult, then, to compare Hungarian kids to American students, almost all of whom were still in school, but far fewer of whom were still taking math.

No one has found a solution to this problem when it comes to testing seniors or, more appropriately phrased, students in their final year of secondary schooling. This phrase is preferable because different nations have quite different systems of sec-

ondary schools. Many students in their final year are not comparable to American high school seniors.

However, today, most countries no longer track students before high school, and most kids in most industrialized nations are in school through the eighth grade and receiving the same instruction. Whether one can build a test that is fair to students in 41 countries — the number of countries that participated in the eighth-grade assessment of the TIMSS — is another question, one not completely resolved.

TIMSS is the largest international study to date. In addition to the 41 nations administering tests to eighth-graders, 26 nations took part at the fourth-grade level, and 24 countries participated in at least some aspect of the TIMSS Final Year Study. This Final Year Study administered four tests: what TIMSS officials called a math literacy test, a science literacy test, an advanced mathematics test, and a physics test. Participating countries were supposed to give the literacy tests to representative samples of students, but they could choose the students they thought appropriate to take the advanced math and physics tests.

To try to solve the selection problems, participating nations provided an organization called Statistics Canada with a list of every school in the nation, along with some demographic characteristics of each school. Statistics Canada specializes in drawing samples, and it provided a list of recommended schools to the countries. TIMSS officials, of course, had no power to compel the countries to use those schools, and some didn't. This proved to be quite a problem in the Final Year Study.

TIMSS officials returned four years later to administer the same tests. This time, 38 nations, 13 U.S. states, and 14 U.S. school districts or consortia of school districts took part.

In the original TIMSS, American fourth-graders finished above average in mathematics and near the top in science. American eighth-graders finished average in both subjects. American 12th-graders *apparently* were at or near the bottom. The operative word, though, is "apparently." These results, unfortunately, were accepted uncritically in many quarters. This acceptance led to the mistaken conclusion that American kids get dumber the longer they stay in school.

I think the drop in performance between fourth grade and eight grade is real, but I also think there is no further drop after that. Why should American students fall behind their international peers between grades 4 and 8? Two basic reasons: 1) American textbooks are huge, and American teachers try to get all the way through them. American textbooks are often three times as thick as those in other nations. In order to teach everything, the teacher can't stay on any one topic for long. Results from another part of the study show that American teachers teach many more topics each year than teachers in other nations. Our kids would score higher if teachers spent more time on fewer topics. 2) For most American students, the middle years are years of reinforcement and review of materials learned earlier. Not many American

kids take algebra in grade 8, though that seems to be changing. Other nations see the middle years as the start of high school and introduce new material. Thus Japanese students receive large injections of algebra in grade 7 and plane geometry at grade 8. American students receive instruction in these subjects in grades 9 and 10, respectively.

The TIMSS Final Year Study has so many problems that space prevents me from detailing them here. I did so in the May 2000 issue of *Educational Researcher.* In general, few countries met the participation and selection criteria established by TIMSS — they eliminated too many of the schools recommended by Statistics Canada or didn't test certain groups in their population (Russia, for instance, tested only Russian-speaking schools). Second, after eighth grade, most American students enter comprehensive high schools. In other nations, they enter special programs. Some go to college-prep schools. In some countries, over half enter vocational programs. The various countries differ in so many ways that comparison is virtually impossible.

In addition, Americans were slighted in part by who participated and in part by culture. On the advanced mathematics test, we tested students taking precalculus as well as those taking calculus. But 23% of the items on the advanced math test *presume* the student has already completed a calculus course. Our precalculus students scored 100 points lower than our students who actually had calculus under their belts. That's what happens when you test kids on stuff they haven't studied. American students who had taken calculus were in the middle of the pack, the same place as American eight- graders.

Moreover, in most countries you are either a worker or a student, not both. But most American seniors *are* both. The research on work and school performance finds that working up to 20 hours a week actually correlates with higher grades. After that, though, the hours of work begin to cut into homework, sleep, and even meals. Yet 27% of American seniors in TIMSS reported working 21-35 hours a week, and another 28% said they worked more than 35 hours a week. American kids who said they worked up to 15 hours a week were at the international average. Those who worked 21-35 hours were much lower; those who worked over 35 dropped off the charts.

There are other problems with the Final Year Study, but these are the most important ones, and they are enough to say, "Disregard this study." I'll just mention one other. My understanding is that other nations don't have a "senior slump" as severe as that found here. Even knowing that, TIMSS tested American seniors in May.

HOW IN THE WORLD DO STUDENTS READ?
American students have consistently done well in international comparisons of reading. In the most recent such comparison, American 9-year-olds were second among students from 27 countries, while American 14-year-olds were eighth among students from 31 nations.[16] At both ages, though, only Finland had a statistically higher score. In addition, the best American readers — those who scored at the 90th, 95th, and 99th percentiles — outscored the entire world.

PISA
In December 2001, the Organisation for Economic Co-operation and Development released its "PISA" study. PISA stands for Program of International Student Assessment. Students in the 28 OECD countries and four others—Liechtenstein, Latvia, Brazil, and the Russian Federation — tested 15-year-olds in reading, mathematics, and science. According to PISA literature, these tests did not measure mastery of school curricula but the ability to apply what had been learned to practical problems.

Germany finished 25th among the 32 nations, and the country's media went ballistic. We could have shipped the German media some of our old head-

lines. Theirs were virtually identical. The calls for reform sound very much like those appearing in 1983 after *A Nation at Risk*, and 1998 after the Final Year report from TIMSS.

For the U.S., the overall results were strictly ho-hum. American students were smack in the middle of the pack in all three areas, very similar to the TIMSS eighth-grade results. As with TIMSS, though, a disaggregation by ethnicity shows that, as far as test scores go, the U.S. maintains two school systems, not one. Here are the ranks attained by various ethnic groups

	Reading	Math	Science
White students	2nd	7th	4th
Black students	29th	30th	30th
Hispanic students	29th	30th	30th

Unfortunately, these results cannot also be disaggregated by poverty levels. Ethnicity probably serves as a good proxy variable for poverty, though.

CHAPTER 5

Specific Tests

So far, we have talked mostly about tests in general. It is worthwhile, though, to discuss a few specific tests that are highly visible and very influential either on life decisions or education policy. We will describe the Iowa Tests of Basic Skills, a commercial norm-referenced achievement test, but this description will suffice to describe achievement tests in general. Most of what is said about the ITBS can be applied to the other widely used achievement tests: the Comprehensive Tests of Basic Skills, the Stanford Achievement Tests, the Metropolitan Achievement Tests, Terra Nova, and California Achievement Tests. Readers can see sample items from many of these tests in *A Parent's Guide to Standardized Tests in School,* by Peter Cookson and Joshua Halberstam. (Some of the text *about* tests, however, contains errors.)

The SAT (known from 1926 to 1996 as the Scholastic Aptitude Test and briefly as the Scholastic Assessment Test) is probably the best known and most widely publicized test of recent years. Its less widely known cousin, the ACT (American College Test) from the American College Testing Program in Iowa City, Iowa, shares most of its features. The tests of the National Assessment of Educational Progress (NAEP) had a low profile for many years but have in recent years strongly affected education policy throughout the nation. A multitude of IQ tests play significant roles in the lives of individuals, and debates about the nature of IQ have reverberated in education circles for almost a century.

THE IOWA TESTS OF BASIC SKILLS

The Iowa Tests of Basic Skills (ITBS) are available for testing children in kindergarten through grade 8. There are two additional sets of "Iowas," as they are often called, that are available for use in high school: the Tests of Achievement and Proficiency and the Iowa Tests of Educational Development.

The latter is a more difficult test with long reading passages, multi-step math problems, and simulated science experiments.

The basic core of the ITBS tests are the vocabulary, reading, language, and mathematics sections. Vocabulary items provide a boldfaced word in the context of a phrase and ask the child to select the word that is most like the boldfaced word. Reading passages include exposition, narrative, and poetry and, according to "A Message to Parents," "Some questions emphasize the understanding of stated information, but most questions require students to make inferences or draw generalizations."

The language section of the test is divided into four sections: spelling, capitalization, punctuation, and usage. In each, items present four lines of text, and the child's task is to pick which line contains an error. The final choice is always *no mistakes* for use with items that are error-free.

Mathematics is divided into math concepts and estimation, problem solving and data interpretation, and computation. These divisions reflect the impact of both the National Council of Teachers of Mathematics Standards and the marketplace. The NCTM standards emphasize reasoning, problem solving, and data interpretation.

Until 1976, the ITBS contained no computation test. The developers of the ITBS at the University of Iowa felt that computation was the test most affected by the sequence of skills learned and most subject to influence from speeded drills. They considered computation something best left to local discretion. However, many states adopt a statewide achievement test by having the various test publishers bid for a contract. The states specify what they want in a test, and the test publishers submit a bid in an effort to convince the state that their test best delivers what the state wants at the lowest price. (Starting in the 1990s a number of states required the companies to develop a test unique to that state's set of educational standards.)

In 1976, Texas and California and several large cities informed the ITBS developers that, if their tests did not contain a computation test, they would not be eligible for adoption. California and Texas combined constitute a huge market. These two states have enough people in them to virtually control what test makers put into their tests, and so the Iowa added a computation test. In the 1980s, the use and scoring of the computation test was made optional to all users.

In addition to this core battery, there are science and social studies subtests and a sources of information test, which is further divided into maps and diagrams and other sources of information. In some tests, including the ITBS, the science and social studies sections contain a great deal of information that the test questions then ask about. This is a tradeoff. By putting the needed information in the material before the questions are asked, students without specific knowledge are not penalized, but the "science" test becomes something more of a "science reading" test.

The ITBS social studies test asks for specific information, such as "Which of these inventions made it practical to construct tall office buildings?" The options are the elevator, the automobile, the glass window, and air conditioning. In science, a question might ask, "Which of these is a body part that helps the animal to catch its food?" The choices are a frog's sticky tongue, a monkey's long tail, a turtle's hard shell, and a lion's thick mane. When the items do provide material, the answer cannot be obtained simply by reading the question. Consider this example:

> Andy poured 75 ml of water into a measuring cup. When he added a stone to the cup, the water level rose to 125 ml. What can be concluded from this information?
>
> A. The water weighs 200 ml.
> B. The stone takes up more space than the water does.
> C. The stone weighs more than the water.
> D. The stone has the same volume as 50 ml of water.

> The SAT is a series of tests that predict your ability to perform in the college environment by measuring the degree to which you possess knowledge that nobody in a million years would actually need.[17] – Dave Barry

The idea behind the question, I imagine, is to test either the student's knowledge that a stone displaces a volume of water equal to its own volume or to test the student's ability to reason it out. However, this is a question that a student could get right without knowing about volume or without reasoning it through. If the student knows what ml stands for, alternatives A and C are eliminated because they deal with weight and weight is not mentioned in the question's stem (the name for the part of the question that presents the information and question). If the student realizes that the level rose 50 ml (from 75 to 125 ml) and realizes that the water took up 75 ml, he can eliminate option B. He thus arrives at the right answer by elimination, never thinking about how objects displace water in the amount of their volume.

The maps and diagrams section shows maps, flow charts, calendars, and so on and asks questions about their content, such as "Mary has to go to the doctor on May 4. What day of the week is that?" The section on sources of information shows tables of contents in various guises.

THE SAT AND THE ACT

Few tests have attained the notoriety that the SAT (formerly Scholastic Assessment Test, nee, Scholastic Aptitude Test) enjoys. It, and its current developer, the Educational Testing Service (ETS), have been the subject of at least three stinging critiques: *The Reign of ETS: The Corporation That Makes Up Minds,* by Allan Nairn and Ralph Nader; *None of the Above,* by David Owen; and *The Case Against the SAT,* by James Crouse and Dale Trusheim. Owen's book is by far the most accessible to the lay reader. Nairn and Nader rely on some peculiar statistics. Crouse and Trusheim's opening and closing chapters are straightforward and readable, but the material in between is highly technical.

Although these books and Dave Barry illustrate some modern opinions about the SAT and its discontents, the SAT began life quietly enough. On 17 November 1900, administrators from some colleges and universities in the Northeast gathered at Columbia University in New York to deal with the problem of high school curricula. The problem was that students were arriving with befuddling high school transcripts. The transcripts often indicated that the students had taken similar courses of study in high school when, in fact, the "same" courses reflected markedly different content. The colleges decided to bring coherence to the high school curriculum by giving tests in various subject areas. The content of the tests would tell high school teachers what the colleges valued. Although only about 3% of high school graduates continued on to college, the colleges had no qualms about making the high schools dance to their tune.

The colleges formed the College Entrance Examination Board to develop, administer, and, initially, score the tests. Although the phrase "measurement-driven instruction" did not become popular until the 1980s, the College Board (as it is usually called) was pushing it almost a century earlier. The College Board did not accomplish its goal.

The College Board soon dropped the scoring service. Colleges complained about having an outside authority determine their standards. How dare they! was pretty much the colleges' reaction. The College Board initially used only essay tests. The first tests were given in 1901 in English,

French, German, Latin, Greek, history, mathematics, and physics, and in the first year 973 students sat for these exams. In the second year, Spanish, botany, geography, and drawing were added, and the number of students rose to 1,362 (in 2001, it was 1,276,320, about 45% of the entire senior class).

Impressed with testing developments during World War I, the College Board decided to develop a more general test that might predict who would succeed in college. In 1926 it presented the world with the Scholastic Aptitude Test (SAT). Its developers were quite modest about its utility. The SAT's principal architect, Carl Campbell Brigham, had this to say about it:

> The present state of all efforts of men to measure or in any way estimate the worth of other men, or to evaluate the results of their nurture, or to reckon their potential possibilities does not warrant any certainty of prediction. . . . This additional test now made available through the instrumentality of the College Entrance Examination Board may help to resolve a few perplexing problems, but it should be regarded merely as a supplementary record. To place too great emphasis on test scores is as dangerous as the failure to properly evaluate any score or rank in conjunction with other measures and estimates which it supplements.

Repeatedly, the College Board has echoed Brigham's words that the SAT "should be regarded merely as a supplementary record." Would that people had kept those words in mind over the years! Actually, for many years the SAT *was* mostly a supplementary record. It was only after a long period of steady declines in SAT national averages that the SAT attained some front-page media attention. (There really is no meaningful "national average" for the SAT. It's a self-selected group that has changed over the years and in the last 20 years has grown from one-third of the high school senior class to 45%.)

From the start, the SAT was divided into two sections, verbal and quantitative. The verbal section consisted of sentence completion, antonyms, analo-gies, and reading comprehension questions. The mathematics section consisted mostly of arithmetic, algebra, and geometry questions. A few questions on the mathematics section were designated as "other" types and included problems in inequalities, logic, intuitive topology, unusual symbols, operations, and definitions. The questions included both essay and multiple-choice items.

The entry of the U.S. into World War II interfered with the administration of the essay portion of the test in 1941, and from that time on the SAT was entirely multiple-choice, consisting of 85 items in the verbal section, 60 in the quantitative. Also in 1941 the College Board adopted a new scale with the average score set at 500 (a standard score, something discussed on pages 67-69) and the standard deviation — the measure of the variability of scores around the average — scaled to 100. All subsequent administrations of the SAT were statistically equated to the 1941 administration in terms of difficulty, until 1996, when the College Board "recentered" the scale for reasons to be discussed momentarily.

It is important to know something about the students who set the original standards on the SAT, standards that were constant until 1996. They were 10,654 students from the Northeast. Ninety-eight percent of them were white, 60% were male, and fully 41% had attended private, college-prep high schools. They were, by all measures, an elite. It was to the average score of this elite that the scaled score of 500 was applied. In 2001 the SAT test-taking seniors consisted of more than one and a quarter million students, 45% of the nation's senior class. In contrast to the standard setters, the class of 2001 was 34% minority, 55% female, 83% public school attendees, 22% from families with incomes of $30,000 or less, and 44% from families with incomes of $50,000 or less.

The pool of SAT test-takers has been truly democratized, but all of these changes are associated with lower test scores. It would have been astonishing — and very suspicious — if the average SAT scores had *not* declined as the test-taking population expanded. More about this later.

By 1950, the SAT verbal score had declined to 476, and it remained very stable around 475 until it began its notorious 20-year descent in 1963. No one speaks of this early decline, probably because no one can explain it. There were no large changes in curriculum between 1941 and 1950. Very few television screens glowed in the nation's living rooms. And in those homes with televisions, 1950 marked the year before the beginning of a new situation comedy, "Ozzie and Harriet." The 1950s, when the scores stayed at the level they had fallen to during the 1940s, were the "togetherness" years of the Eisenhower Administration, the years of *The Organization Man* and *The Man in the Gray Flannel Suit.* Few people worried about the decline of the family. Only jazz musicians and a few other marginalized groups regularly used illegal drugs. Thus three powerful factors invoked to explain later declines — drugs, TV, and family disintegration — could not be invoked to explain the first SAT score slide.

My guess is that it had something to do with the G.I. Bill, which permitted people to attend college who otherwise could not have afforded it. But we will never know for certain. In those days the College Board did not collect the kind of data it now gathers with the "Self Descriptive Questionnaire" that now accompanies the SAT.

In any case, *both* the verbal and quantitative scores began to decline in 1963 and fell for 20 years. In 1977 the College Board put together a panel to study the falling scores. The panel, headed by Willard Wirtz, former U.S. Secretary of Labor, and Harold Howe II, former U.S. Commissioner of Education, concluded that most of the decline from 1963 to 1970 was the result of changes in who was taking the test: more women, more minorities, more lower-income students, and more students with mediocre high school grades. But, the panel claimed, those changes had stabilized by 1970, and other reasons needed to be found to explain the rest

of the decline (some of the panel's technical staff disagreed that the demographics were stable in this second half of the decline.)

And did the panel ever find those reasons! One background paper for the panel simply listed the hypotheses that had been brought forward to explain the drop, all 76 of them. This works out to roughly one hypothesis for each point of the decline. And the paper missed one of my favorites: that the decline occurred because of radioactive fallout from the nuclear testing program of the 1940s and 1950s (some have suggested that the article with this proposal was a satire).

Changes in curriculum, in teachers, in students, in the family, in religion, in civil rights, in values, in national priorities, in the economy, and in technology were all presented as candidates for causing the decline in SAT scores. The panel elected to go with some large societal disturbances in what it referred to as "a decade of distraction." Whether or not the demographics of test-takers were stable in the 1970s, the 1980s and 1990s brought large changes. Increasing numbers of Asian, Hispanic, black, and low-income students began to huddle in angst to bubble in answer sheets on Saturday mornings. When I conducted an analysis that took these changes in population into account, I determined that the verbal test had fallen only 22 points since 1951, while the quantitative, now usually referred to as the math section, had not declined at all.[18]

Even without taking demographics into account, the mathematics section never showed a large decline. It fell only into the 470s. Given the number of questions on the math section, this means that the average student in, say, 1983 when the decline ended, was getting about three fewer of the 60 items correct than in 1941. The fall in the SAT verbal from 1963 to 1983 represented about seven items (starting from the 475 in 1950).

If one accepts the decline without taking into account any demographic changes, the evidence still indicates that the test score decline affected *only* the college-going population. All during the period when the SAT was falling, scores on the PSAT (Preliminary SAT) were stable. Now the PSAT is a short version of the SAT that is usually taken by high school sophomores and juniors. Periodically, ETS conducts a national norming study on a representative sample of all students. The SAT declined from 1963 to 1983, but the PSAT national norming studies from 1964 to 1983 show no indication of change. In a national norming study, recall, students are selected so as to be representative of the whole nation. The SAT is taken only by those aspiring to attend college, and there is some indication that, as more and more students acquired such aspirations, the college-bound curriculum in high school was somewhat watered down.

Conservative school critics have used another aspect of the SAT score decline as evidence that public education is in crisis. Average scores fell, but so did the proportion of students scoring above 650 on the SAT verbal. That group made up about 7% of the standard-setting group but just over 3% of the test-takers in the mid-1970s. It has crept up to about 4% since then. Some of this decline, no doubt, occurred because a larger and larger proportion of the senior class has been taking the SAT. If one assumes that those scoring very high were always among those who were headed for college, then the increasing number of test-takers would be made up mostly of less able students, and those who score high would constitute a smaller proportion of this larger pool.

However, the absolute numbers of high scorers also fell. For instance, in 1966 and 1975, very similar numbers of students took the SAT. In 1966, 33,200 scored above 700 on the SAT verbal, but in 1975, only 15,900 had such high scores. By 1995, the last year in which the old scale was used, the number was down to 12,800, but about 35% fewer students took the SAT in 1995 than in 1975. If the 1975 and 1995 groups had had the same number of test-takers, the 1995 would have had 17,000 students scoring above 700, a slight increase over 1975, but still less than 1966.

Notice that all of the discussion of the decline of high scorers has been limited to the verbal section of the SAT. That is because the proportion of students scoring high on the quantitative section never declined much and, since 1981, has rebounded to become a record large group. In 1981, some 7% of the students were above 650, about the same as in the standard-setting group. By 2001, though, the proportion had grown every year but one and had nearly doubled to 13.4%.

Some people have credited high-scoring Asian and Asian American students for this rise. It is not clear what point they are trying to make, but in any case they are wrong. In 1995, I analyzed growth in high SAT scorers by ethnicity. Asian students do score much higher on the quantitative section of the SAT than any other ethnic group. In 2001, they averaged 566. Whites, the second-highest group, averaged 531. No other group averaged above 500.

However, Asians constitute too small a proportion of the test population to account for much of the growth. Between 1981 and 1995, the proportion of students scoring above 650 on the quantitative section of the SAT grew by about 75%. If the "Asian math gene" hypothesis is true and if Asian students are removed from test-taking group, that 75% increase should disappear or at least become quite small. However, with Asians held out of the sample, the proportion of high scorers still grows by at 57%, so a lot more black, white, Hispanic, and Native American kids are scoring high in math, too. By 2001, the proportion of high scorers had grown 90% overall since 1981 and 67% with Asian students removed from the sample.

Such growth makes sense when one looks at the statistics for course-taking in mathematics and science: many more students in recent years have taken three and four years of these subjects than they did 15 years ago.

I have referred above to the "old scale" and to the "recentering" that took place in 1996. You might be wondering what this is all about. Recall that since 1941 demographic changes meant that 500 no

> Eighty percent of what determines who makes dean's list and who gets slapped with academic probation must come from sources other than what the SAT measures.

longer represented the score of the average college applicant. By 1996, 62% of all high school graduates were enrolled in some form of higher education in the following fall. The College Board decided to "recenter" the SAT scale to reflect this changed population. The publishers of achievement tests do this every time they renorm a test. The different term was probably occasioned by the College Board's twin desires to be unique and to garner as much media coverage as possible.

The College Board wanted 500 to once again represent the performance of the average test-taker. Using the 1941 scale, students receiving a score of 475 would naturally think that they were below average. And they were — but only in comparison to the 1941 elite who set the original standards. The recentering generated a storm of protest from conservative school critics. Former assistant secretary of education Chester Finn, Jr., called it the "biggest dose of educational Prozac" ever administered. Others claimed that the College Board was trying to hide low achievement.

I think the critics were off target. If you want the average score of the SAT to reflect the score of the average student taking the test, the recentering makes sense.

Does the SAT work? Well, before we can answer that question, we have to know exactly what it is supposed to do. The SAT is supposed to predict

success in the freshman year of college. Does it? Yes, but not as well as the College Board and the ETS would have you believe. In one study, the SAT successfully predicted freshman grade-point averages no better than the scores from achievement tests. And high school grade-point averages are better predictors at most universities.

The SAT is not really a very powerful predictor of college grades. The typical correlation between SAT scores and freshman grades is around .45. This means that the SAT accounts for only 20% of what goes into freshman grades. (The amount of variance in one variable that can be explained by another is given by the square of the correlation coefficient: .45 x .45= .2025.) That means that 80% of what determines who makes dean's list and who gets slapped with academic probation must come from sources other than what the SAT measures.

Beyond the freshman year, the SAT's predictive powers fall off markedly, and no one — not even the College Board — claims that SAT scores have any relationship to life after college. "If you're interested in creativity or who's going to make a difference on their jobs, SAT scores are not good predictors," says Yale University psychology and education professor Robert Sternberg. Naturally, the College Board has not been particularly interested in checking out the accuracy of Sternberg's claim.

Results from some schools that have made SAT scores optional for admission purposes also raise questions about its value. These schools make the SAT optional as part of the admissions process, but require SAT scores *after* admission for research, guidance, and placement purposes. Thus all students at these schools have SAT scores, but some didn't use them as part of their admissions application, and others did.

Students who submit their SATs as part of their admissions package score about 150 total points higher than those who don't submit them. But — and it's a big but — their college grade-point averages don't differ from the SAT submitters, and those who do not submit SATs don't leave school for academic reasons at any higher rate than those who sent their SATs to the dean of admissions. The nonsubmitters have turned out to be a more diverse group of applicants in terms of geographic area, ethnicity, and intended major (fine arts and performing arts majors are not typically great paper-and-pencil test-takers). Moreover, the faculties at the colleges that have abandoned the SAT have pronounced themselves better satisfied with the more diverse student bodies that have resulted. (Think about it: a college full of high scorers on the SAT would be a pretty awful environment; even colleges like Stanford and Harvard have a number of students with total scores of under 900.)

Is the SAT biased? There have been claims that the SAT is biased against both women and minorities. The notion of bias against ethnic groups or lower socioeconomic status students arose over vocabulary words in the test like "regatta." A regatta is more likely to be a part of the culture of affluent people, and knowing what the word means is more likely to reflect a milieu of cultural privilege than an aptitude for college. There are statistical procedures for determining bias, and in recent years the claims of ethnic bias have died down.

If claims of ethnic bias are fewer these days, the gap between whites and Asians on the one hand and blacks and Hispanics on the other remains a source of concern. Indeed, in 2000, Richard Atkinson, president of the University of California, called for the abolition of the SAT at that university. Atkinson sought to replace the SAT with the College Board's Achievement Tests in specific subjects until something else could be developed. It is not likely, however, that any test-based system will reduce the inequities. Nor would the use of grades — the disparities are almost as great with this measure.

Some states are moving to an admissions system where the top, say, 10% of students at all schools in the state are admitted to the state university system. (Iowa has had this system for many years; anyone in the top half of the class can attend the state university system.) This has drawn howls

from conservative critics who equate the SAT with "merit." But, as we saw in the list of characteristics that tests don't measure, there is much more to a human being than academic achievement. We also saw above that colleges that no longer require the SAT get students who achieve just as well in college. Equating high SAT scores with general merit simply won't wash.

Claims of gender bias endure. No one really knows why women score lower on the SAT than men, even on the verbal section, but they do. The difference on the verbal score is tiny, four or five points each year on the SAT's 600-point scale. The difference in math is much larger, 35 to 40 points depending on year. In 2001, males averaged 509 on the verbal; females, 502. On the math, males averaged 533; females, 498.

The difference also shows up on the PSAT, and that difference has an important practical outcome: the PSAT is the sole instrument by which students qualify for the National Merit Scholarship Program. Each year, about two-thirds of these scholarships go to males. This would be of no import if the higher SAT scores of males were followed by higher grade-point averages in college, but they aren't. One large study found a difference of 45 points on the SAT math section between males and females, but mostly small differences in college freshman math grades in favor of females, no matter whether the freshman math course was remedial, standard college, advanced algebra, or calculus.

The people who run the National Merit Scholarship Program have been singularly unresponsive to pleas to change the award process. They have refused to consider changes, even though it has been pointed out that, once we get to the semi-finalist level of selecting students, we are dealing with achievement levels so high that the prizes could be given *at random* and the quality of the students getting the awards would not decline. But, because the National Merit organization is private and accepts no public money, it can do what it wants.

> The College Board and ETS have for many years promulgated the myth that the SAT can serve as a "common yardstick" for all students.

Is the SAT a life-determining test? Yes, said Nicholas Lemann in *The Big Test*. No, said I in my *Washington Post* review of Lemann's book (reprinted at the back of this book). Lemann described the SAT as "the all-powerful bringer of individual destiny in the United States." I said, "Get serious." I showed that selective colleges could fill their freshmen classes with students garnering 1500 total points or more — but they don't. Indeed, elite schools regularly turn down hundreds of students with perfect 1600 SAT scores. They give weight to many other factors. The press made a big deal over Mount Holyoke's abandoning the SAT in 2000, but Holyoke President Joanne Creighton pointed out that it had never counted for more than 10% in admissions decisions.

The public, though, believes Lemann is right. A cartoon about the time Lemann's book was published showed a mother reading to her child in bed. The mother says, "And the little pig with the higher math and verbal scores lived happily ever after. The other two were swallowed by the wolf."

Given the *perceived* importance of the SAT in college admissions, the question arises: Can the SAT be coached? Certainly two large corporations, Kaplan, Inc., and The Princeton Review, Inc., claim that it can be. Unfortunately but understandably, these two firms have not produced the kinds of evidence that researchers will accept, nor have they been willing to permit researchers to conduct the kinds of experimental studies that would resolve the issue one way or another.

I mentioned earlier that psychometricians sometimes act more like members of a religious order than like scientists. When I worked at ETS in the 1960s, the true believers considered the SAT's imperviousness to coaching as revealed truth. When an ETS researcher showed that coaching could indeed raise scores, ETS fired him.

Whether or not the SAT is coachable depends in part on how one defines "coaching." Most short-term instruction over a week or so probably has little impact other than to revive dormant skills learned earlier (e.g., a number of SAT math problems look impossible until one remembers a trick, and they then become quite simple). The Princeton Review claims that its methods work by teaching students the "games" that ETS plays in item construction. I imagine this helps a little. Kaplan relies more on prolonged contact with SAT and SAT-like material. A hard-to-answer question is, When does "prolonged contact" cease to be coaching and become instruction?

Some item types would appear to be more coachable than others. Learning words and their antonyms, for instance, no doubt has little impact because of the small probability of encountering any specific word. On the other hand, practice in analogies might lead to the development of a more general skill. It would certainly teach a few "games." Most people approach analogies by seeking to solve them in terms of meaning, but for some analogy problems, meaning is irrelevant. For instance pool:sleep as ?: peels. The alternatives might be loop, pool, sloop, spool. "Peels" is "sleep" reversed, so the answer would be "loop," which is "pool" reversed.

The College Board and ETS have for many years promulgated the myth that the SAT can serve as a "common yardstick" for all students. After all, it is a standardized test, and everyone takes it under the same circumstances, while high school grades from the Bronx High School of Science and from South

Succotash High don't reflect the same level of attainment (or might not, at least). The latter point is true, but it is also true that, despite this lack of comparability, the high school records of students from all over the country predict college success better than the SAT. Indeed, the best predictor is the grade-point average on what are termed the rigorous courses in high school: mathematics, sciences, and advanced courses in English and the social sciences.

The myth of the "common yardstick" is silly on its face. The test might be standardized, but the kids who take it are not. It's instructive to repeat here an example from the answers to the quiz given in the first chapter. Suppose we have one applicant to college who comes from a wealthy, college-educated family, attends an elite college-prep high school, and scores 600 on the SAT verbal. Suppose we have another student who lives in an inner city with poor parents who never completed high school, attends the neighborhood public school, lacks a quiet place to study, works to help the family make ends meet, and scores 600 on the SAT verbal. Are these two students the same? Of course not. And college admissions officers know it. They will recruit the inner-city student like crazy and give the college-prep kid a ho-hum response (unless the parents are either wealthy or alumni or preferably both).

The "common yardstick" myth also serves to perpetuate another fiction: that all applicants to a college are in competition with all other applicants. This has never been so. Colleges admit by categories: the brains, the all-American kids, the special talents (athletes, artists, actors, musicians, etc.), the social conscience (perhaps an endangered species as more state laws forbid affirmative action), the legacies (offspring of alumni), and the paying guests (those who don't need scholarship help).

Finally, state-level SAT results have been used to "prove" that money doesn't matter. Former secretary of education William Bennett made such a claim in a "Report Card on American Education," issued by a conservative think tank. *Washington Post* pundit and fellow conservative George Will pounced on the results with a column headlined, "Meaningless Money Factor." Will pointed out that the top five states — Iowa, North Dakota, South Dakota, Utah, and Minnesota — all ranked low in spending for public education. New Jersey, on the other hand, spent more money per kid per year than any other state and still only finished 39th in the Great SAT Race. What neither Will nor Bennett bothered to point out was that in the high-scoring states, very few students take the SAT: they are all states that principally use the ACT. The percentages of students taking the SAT for the five states in the year of the study were 5, 6, 5, 4, and 10, respectively.

The kids in Iowa who take the SAT are kids who want to leave Iowa and attend Harvard, Stanford, or some other highly selective school that requires the SAT. In New Jersey, on the other hand, fully 76% of the senior class take the test. It doesn't take a genius to realize that if one state sends a 5% elite to compete against three-fourths of the student body, the elite is gonna look good.

Will might or might not have known about the differences in rates across states. Bennett most assuredly did. It is depressing to see the author of *The Book of Virtues* being so cavalier about two of them, honesty and truth.

When a couple of researchers analyzed state-level SAT data, taking into account the differences in participation rates, they found that the differences in participation rates accounted for 83% of the differences in SAT scores among the states. They also found that when participation rates were taken into account, SAT scores rose by 15 points for every thousand dollars above the national average that a state spent on its schools.

What about that other test, the ACT, from the American College Testing Program? Much of what has been said above about the SAT applies to the ACT as well. The ACT is another college admissions battery, developed in the 1950s by the

American College Testing Program in Iowa. It differed from the SAT in that it tested more areas: reading, mathematics, science reading, and social studies reading. The latter two subjects have since been dropped. Its items were more like those on achievement tests, although the SAT has now altered its items to bring them into closer alignment with the high school curriculum. The ACT also took more of a counseling and guidance focus in some of the background questions it asked students.

According to an ETS memo cited in Lemann's book, ETS officials felt that they would deal with an elite while the ACT would handle the "great unwashed." This glib and condescending characterization reflects a genuine difference in the beginnings of the two organizations. ETS wanted to scan the country for geniuses who could make it at Ivy League schools. ACT was looking to find those who could not cope with college and to help both the college-bound and rest find appropriate postsecondary activities.

The ACT exhibited a decline similar to that of the SAT. Less attention has been paid to it for reasons of history, geography, and psychology. The SAT is a much older test, and it was developed in the East where more people live. But most important, the College Board and ETS have both been very energetic and successful in seeking attention from the media. The ACT people working out in Iowa have almost shunned media attention.

THE NATIONAL ASSESSMENT OF EDUCATIONAL PROGRESS (NAEP)

For many years NAEP was practically invisible. This was a legacy of the political battles to establish it at all. In 1994, I learned of someone writing her doctoral dissertation on the history of NAEP, a topic I was also working on at the time. I called her, and, in our ensuing correspondence, she apologized for being so enthusiastic about the topic. But, she said, "It is rare that have I the opportunity to talk to anyone who has even *heard* of NAEP." Since 1994, it has become much better known.

NAEP was the brainchild of Francis Keppel, U.S. Commissioner of Education in the 1960s. Keppel was impressed with how much the collection of health statistics had improved the health of Americans simply by calling attention to the rates of certain diseases. If you don't know how many cases of tuberculosis there are, it's hard to know how much of an effort you need to mount to eradicate it.

Keppel didn't think the American education system was very healthy, and he wanted a means of demonstrating its pathologies to the public at large. Keppel asked Ralph Tyler, an educator and at the time director of the Institute for Advanced Studies in the Behavioral Sciences at Stanford University, to undertake the project. Tyler, in turn, formed alliances with various testing companies.

Remember that the goal of a norm-referenced test is to spread people out in order to make discriminations and differential predictions, while the goal of a criterion-referenced test is to hold performance up to some standard. Tyler had yet another notion of how to use a test. Tyler's idea for NAEP was simply to find out what is and what isn't — just as with health statistics. What do our kids know and what don't they know? To this end, Tyler thought NAEP should ask some questions that half of the students would know, as with a norm-referenced test. But it should also ask some questions that people felt almost everyone (90%) would know and some questions that virtually no one (10%) would be able to answer correctly. This would reveal what most people know, what some people know, and what most people don't know.

Tyler's logic went like this:

> The need for data on progress has been recognized in other spheres of American life. During the depression the lack of dependable information about the progress of the economy was a serious handicap in focusing efforts and in assessing their impact. Out of this need grew an index of production, Gross National Product, which has been of great value in guid-

ing economic development. Correspondingly, the Consumer Price Index was developed as a useful measure of the changes in the cost of living and inflation. Education, today, is of great concern to all Americans. Without education our young people cannot get jobs, are unable to participate intelligently and responsibly in civic and social life, and fail to achieve individual self realization. Education is increasingly recognized as the servant of all our purposes.[19]

Therefore, Tyler argued, we need to know how well our servant is serving us. Keppel agreed with Tyler, although he was more interested in having our servant serve us better.

Before Keppel and Tyler got NAEP off the drawing board, virtually every education organization in the nation and number of members of Congress as well, attacked the very idea of NAEP. The National Education Association (NEA), the American Association of School Administrators (AASA), and the Association for Supervision and Curriculum Development (ASCD) all mounted blistering offensives against the concept. They argued that NAEP would stultify innovation, impede equal opportunity, bring pressure on administrators and teachers, and encourage cheating.

Most of all, though, organizations opposed NAEP because they saw it as "the camel's nose under the tent," which would inexorably be followed by the whole camel — a federally written and controlled curriculum. The education establishment of the day viewed a federal test as the first step towards the loss of local control. Local control of education was an even more treasured aspect of public schools then than it is today.

In order to get NAEP off the ground, Tyler and his colleagues had to agree not to report state- or district-level results. NAEP would issue reports for the nation, for regions (e.g., the Northeast), and for urban and rural areas. This reduced NAEP's utility to zero except for tracking national trends. In 1988, Congress amended the law to permit state-by-state

comparisons. Currently, about 40 states participate in state-level NAEP. NAEP also presents results by parental education level, by ethnicity, by free-lunch eligibility, and by type of school (public, Catholic, other private).

From the beginning, NAEP attempted to devise novel forms of test items. Of course, some were multiple-choice questions, and some remain that way today, but open-ended questions were also employed. NAEP continues today to be a mixture of multiple-choice and open-ended items.

The original contract for NAEP was awarded to the Education Commission of the States (ECS), a policy-tracking body based in Denver, Colorado. ECS, as an organization sponsored by state governors, was seen as a safe place for NAEP, keeping it away from the influence of federal agencies. Initially, ECS was awarded the NAEP contract on a "sole source" basis — i.e., no other organization could compete for the contract. As NAEP expanded, pressure grew to award the relatively lucrative contract by competitive bid, the way most contracts are let. In 1982, as a result of just such a competition, the contract for NAEP passed from the ECS to ETS. ETS launched an effort to make NAEP more visible by referring to it as "The Nation's Report Card."

NAEP still remains out of sight of most people because there is no feedback below the state level. Teachers never know how their charges did — nor do the students or their parents or anyone else. Although it has not been documented by research, many people feel that, because NAEP has no significance to anyone's life, people don't take it seriously. When a district in which I worked in Colorado participated in a NAEP state-level field test, about half of the teachers involved reported to me that they had trouble keeping the students on task.

It seems likely, therefore, that NAEP systematically underestimates the level of achievement displayed by American school children. As Archie Lapointe, the former executive director of NAEP once told me, the big problem with NAEP is keeping kids awake during the test. And motivated students score much higher than listless ones.

After the appearance of *A Nation at Risk* in 1983, the political appointees of the U.S. Department of Education began to seek a new use for NAEP scores. Whereas Tyler and his colleagues had seen NAEP only in descriptive terms, showing what students did and did not know, others — notably Chester Finn, Jr., former assistant secretary of education — wished to use NAEP prescriptively: to provide information about what students know on subjects that students *should* know.

To this end, Finn, as the chairman of the National Assessment Governing Board (NAGB, pronounced NAG-bee) gathered groups of people together to rate the levels of the items and establish standards by which students would be placed at levels called "basic, proficient, and advanced." The first round of such standard setting produced a set of standards that indicated that virtually no students had skills that would permit them to cope with college-level material and indicated as well that many students did not have the skills to function at the grades in which they found themselves. Although NAGB wished to use the standards to sustain the sense of crisis that had been created by *A Nation at Risk,* the standards it set were so high that they seemed outlandish even to NAGB's ideologues.

Another round of standard setting resulted in slightly lower but still exceptionally high standards. These standards had their problems, too. A team of well-known evaluators hired by NAGB to evaluate both the standard-setting process and the standards themselves pronounced the standards "technically indefensible."[20] NAGB summarily fired the team. Or, at least, it tried to. The contract forbid such arbitrary action. Other reviews of the standards by the Center for Research in Evaluation, Standards, and Student Testing; by the U.S. General Accounting Office; and by the National Academy of Education also found the standards problematical. The National Academy declared that

the standards should come with a "warning label" pronouncing them "suggestive," not "definitive." The National Research Council called them "fundamentally flawed."

Still, politicians, ideologues, the media, and even some educators take the standards as given, and it is not hard to find people clucking over such "facts" as this: "Only 7½% of our three million high school seniors leave their secondary school experience with an ability to integrate scientific information with other knowledge." Even Bill Clinton got into the act, declaring that "only 40% of our third-graders can read independently." This last "fact" was based on a rather loose interpretation of the NAEP levels, but it served as the basis for Clinton's proposal for a "voluntary" national test in reading and mathematics (precisely what NAEP's original opponents had feared 30 years earlier).

Numerous problems afflict the NAEP achievement levels. First, according to the NAEP procedures and the associated rhetoric, if a student tests at particular level in, say, mathematics, then we should be able to specify what kinds of math problems he will get right and what kinds he will get wrong. But it doesn't work out that way. The various studies mentioned above found that students at a particular level of mathematics get some items right that they ought not to be able to cope with and get some items wrong that they ought to be able to do easily.

Second, NAEP labels such as "advanced" lack any precise meaning, because they are not linked to anything else in the world. Consider, by contrast, the statement that "in order to have a 50-50 chance of passing college algebra, you have to score at X level on the ACT college admissions tests." This "level" on the ACT is linked to a real-world event: passing college algebra. And it is linked to that real-world event because the psychometricians at ACT followed 250,000 high school seniors through their college careers in order to see how students with different scores fared. From a score on the ACT tests, they can predict the likelihood that a student will earn a passing grade in college algebra (and, of course, in other college courses). This gives their levels an anchor that is missing from NAEP.

Indeed, it is not possible to link NAEP with other outcomes for individuals. Because NAEP wants to ask a wide variety of questions but it doesn't want to take up a lot of class time, no student takes an entire NAEP test. All students take only certain portions. Of course, all items are given to enough students so that NAEP can estimate what proportion of students nationwide would get any particular item right. But no student ever has a score for the whole test.

Lacking a test score tied to particular students, we cannot track any individual to see whether the "advanced-level" students do that much better than the students who were merely "proficient." Thus the levels have no firm connection to reality and are of questionable validity. It is a curiosity to me that so many people are willing to say harshly negative things about the NAEP levels in private but not in public.

Third, and most important, among the failings of the achievement levels, the results they yield do not accord with other data. For instance, in the 1996 NAEP science assessment, only 29% of fourth-graders scored at or above the proficient level, and a mere 3% scored at the advanced level. Yet in the Third International Mathematics and Science Study (TIMSS), American fourth-graders were third in the world among students from 26 nations. Similarly, in the 1998 NAEP reading assessment, only 31% of the students were proficient or better, and only 7% were advanced. Yet, in another international comparison, American fourth-graders finished second only to Finland in a study of 27 nations. (These results are discussed in more detail in the section on international tests, p. 42-45). If American students show so well when compared to students in other nations, how can they seem so poor on NAEP? The answer is in the achievement levels, not the kids.

IQ TESTS

No tests have caused more controversy than IQ tests, so it certainly behooves us to know something about them. IQ tests originated in France at the beginning of the 20th century, when the French Ministry of Education assigned a clinical psychologist, Alfred Binet, the task of constructing tests that would identify children who could not benefit from normal schooling. Binet, a kindly and humane sort, struggled with his assignment, knowing that his tests would have life-altering outcomes for some of the children who did poorly on them. Recall that tests as we know them did not exist then. Binet was essentially starting from scratch.

Among the things that Binet did was to ask teachers what kinds of tasks caused their students the most difficulty. And he developed at least some of his tests from such considerations. Thus it should not have surprised anyone that students who scored low on the tests would have difficulty in school, since teachers had already said that these tasks caused difficulties.

In the end, Binet concluded that the nature of the individual tests was not all that important. What was important was that there were a lot of them. In 1911 he wrote that "a particular test isolated from the rest is of little value; . . . that which gives a demonstrative force is a group of tests. . . . One test signifies nothing, let us emphatically repeat, but five or six tests signify something." Binet was developing a concept later referred to as "intelligence in general."

If a student did poorly on a given test, that wouldn't be so bad if she did better on another five or so tests. None of the tests held any more value for Binet than any of the others. If one student did well on tests 1, 2, 3, 4, and 5, but not 6, that was the same for Binet as another student who did well on tests 1, 2, 3, 5, and 6, but not 4.

This equivalence for Binet was emphasized by a concept he developed and called "mental age." Binet reasoned that, for the tests to be useful, children should do better as they got older. So he developed a system for classifying the tests according their mental age. A test was said to have a mental age of, say, 6, if 80% to 90% of the 6-year-olds could complete it successfully. Suppose that 90% of 6-year-olds performed a particular test successfully. Suppose as well that smaller percentages of 4- and 5-year-olds and larger percentages of and 7- and 8-year-olds performed successfully, then that test was said to have a mental age of 6.

Binet also decided, somewhat arbitrarily, to have each of his tests count for six months of mental age. This was as far as Binet went with his scaling, placing the tests at various positions on his scale of mental age and summing the number of tests passed to obtain an individual child's mental age. The first scales appeared in 1905, with revisions in 1908 and 1911. The 1905 scale was "normed" on about 50 children deemed normal, while the 1908 scale used some 300 such children; the 1911 scale was a minor revision. While Binet incorporated some tests that involved sensory and perceptual tasks, his scales emphasized verbal functioning, especially judgment, comprehension, and reasoning.

It was not long before a German psychologist, Wilhelm Stern, pointed out that by itself a mental age of, say, 8, was ambiguous. Its meaning depended greatly on the person's chronological age. A 5-year-old with a mental age of 8 would be quite advanced; a 12-year-old with the same mental age would be quite backward. Stern suggested that Binet divide the mental age by the chronological age and multiply by 100 to get rid of the decimals. For a 5-year-old, this means 8/5, yielding a quotient of 1.6, which, multiplied by 100, yields 160. For a 12-year-old, this means 8/12, yielding a quotient of .67, which, multiplied by 100, yields 67. Stern suggested that this quotient be called the Intelligence Quotient or IQ.

Later on, other psychometricians pointed out that the intelligence quotient, as a genuine quotient, had troublesome statistical properties of its own. A child of 5 with a mental age of 8 would get an IQ

of 160. A child of 10 with a mental age of 13 would get an IQ of 130. Yet, in terms of mental age, both children would be three years ahead of their chronological age. This problem was "solved" by using what is called the "deviation IQ." At all age levels, raw scores are converted into standard scores with a mean of 100 and a standard deviation of 15 (see pages 71-73 for a discussion of standard deviations and pages 67-69 for standard scores).

A child who has the median score for his chronological age gets an IQ of 100. A child who is one standard deviation above the mean gets an IQ of 115 (the standard deviation having been set arbitrarily at 15). And so forth.

When Binet's notion of "intelligence in general" crossed the Atlantic, it underwent a curious transformation and became "general intelligence." Binet had warned that many tests were necessary to capture the complexity of "intelligence in general." But the notion of "general intelligence" suggested a more singular, unitary concept that affected all aspects of life.

The idea that intelligence might be a single entity dovetailed nicely with the rediscovery of Mendelian genetics, which suggested that very complex traits could be controlled by a single gene. Thus three ideas converged to cause a great deal of excitement in the early testing community in the U.S.: 1) intelligence influences every aspect of life, 2) intelligence is a unitary entity controlled by a single gene, and 3) IQ tests measure intelligence.

To these early psychometricians — Robert Yerkes, Carl Campbell Brigham, H. H. Goddard, and Lewis Terman (who had developed Binet's scales into something he called the Stanford-Binet IQ Test) — these three ideas opened up the possibility of a nearly ideal society, a society in which the rewards that society offered would be justly distributed to those who were most deserving: namely, those who were the most intelligent. No longer would people be able to say, "If you're so smart, why aren't you rich?"

Aside from the fact that the ideas are all eminently challengeable, the big problem with the early testing movement was that the psychometricians involved were both hereditarians and racists. They also believed, with the strength of religious conviction, that they were right. Indeed, they knew they were right. I stress this point because, even today, psychometricians are influenced by this legacy and sometimes act more like members of a religious order than members of a disinterested scientific society.

Although it was Kelly who invented the multiple-choice format that permitted the mass testing of groups and although it was Terman who developed the famous Stanford-Binet IQ test, it was Goddard who was the most politically active and influential and enthusiastic of the early testers. In the early 1920s, he would go down from his upper-Manhattan office at Columbia University to meet the boats at Ellis Island and administer IQ tests to immigrants. He had no compunction about declaring that at least three-fourths of those landing at the time — largely Poles, Czechs, Hungarians, Italians, Greeks, Slavs, and Eastern European Jews — were mentally unfit.

It apparently never occurred to Goddard that many of these new arrivals had not attended school or had not ever held a pencil in their hands until he thrust one at them. He never questioned the translators' ability to create a valid test in another language on the spot. Nevertheless, Goddard prevailed in promulgating his conclusion that the new arrivals, many from Eastern and Southern Europe, were not nearly as bright as the Northern European immigrants who had preceded them. He convinced Congress to roll back the immigration quotas to the 1890 numbers that were much more favorable to those from the nations of Northern Europe. In 1924 President Coolidge signed the legislation saying, "After all, America must be kept safe for Americans."

Goddard and the others also thought that American society had already done a pretty good job of

> The big problem with the early testing movement was that the psychometricians involved were both hereditarians and racists.

sorting people out by ability. "The people who are doing drudgery are, as a rule, in their proper places," he said.[21] He told an audience of Princeton freshmen:

> Now the fact is, that workmen may have a 10-year intelligence while you have a 20. To demand for him such a home as you enjoy is as absurd as it would be to insist that every laborer should receive a graduate fellowship. How can there be such a thing as social equality with this wide range of mental capacity?

Elsewhere, Goddard made it clear how the new social order was to be created. "Democracy means that the people rule by selecting the wisest, most intelligent to tell them what to do to be happy. Thus Democracy is a method for arriving at a truly benevolent aristocracy."

This was hardly a new idea in American society. Centuries before tests, Thomas Jefferson had proposed a program of education for the state of Virginia that would sort out each year the best minds and allow them to continue their education at state expense. (Those who could afford it could send their children of whatever talent to school for as long as they liked.) Instead of a test, Jefferson's plan called for a "visitor" to visit each school and pick the smartest kids. Jefferson claimed that "by this mean twenty of the best geniuses will be raked from the rubbish annually. . . ." In this way, Jefferson thought, we would arrive at an "aristocracy of worth and genius," in contrast to the European aristocracy that was solely determined by the accident of birth. Although Jefferson clearly didn't think that all men were created equal in the mental realm, he did hold that intelligence was equally distributed among rich and poor classes. Goddard would have said that Jefferson labored under a terrible delusion.

Against the psychometricians' arguments that IQ was determined by genes — nature — there arose another school of psychologists who claimed that intelligence was strongly affected by the environment — nurture. The nature/nurture controversy has seesawed back and forth ever since the earliest claims of the psychometricians. And it continues today. At times it seems to favor genes; at other times, the environment.

In 1995 *The Bell Curve* made a forceful — but not entirely sound — argument in favor of nature. A recent study, much touted by both Bill and Hillary Clinton, indicates the importance of infantile stimulation in the development of connections in the brain, a finding strongly in favor of nurture. Studies of impoverished youths who received cognitively oriented instruction in preschools have found that such instruction has positive influences that can be seen well into adulthood on such indicators as graduation rates, arrest rates, marriage stability, and home ownership, to mention just a few.

As an either/or proposition, the nature/nurture debate is silly. And false. Obviously, both are important. Part of the reason that the evident silliness of the debate has remained obscure is that those on different sides have taken strong stances. Those on different of the argument have also cited different kinds of research evidence to support their claims. Naturists use correlational research; nurturists use experimental data.

To see the difference this makes, let us perform the following hypothetical experiment. Let us assume, for the sake of argument, that we have six sets of parents. Both parents in each pair have the same tested IQ (we'll ignore the possibility of "measurement error"). Let us give each set of parents a set of identical twins. The genetic makeup of such twins is identical; thus their "nature" is identical. Each set of parents gets to raise one twin, and we assume that the parents will act in ways that will tend to make the child have an IQ similar to theirs. The other twin is raised by other parents coached by psychologists and educators who provide the kind of intellectual, cognitive stimulation that seems likely to increase IQ; thus the nurture of the second twin is quite different from that of the first. At the end of six years (about as early as a child's IQ becomes stable enough to rely on), we measure the IQ of our sets of twins. The results are shown below.

	Parent IQ	Twin 1 IQ	Twin 2 IQ
Parents 1	100	100	150
Parents 2	101	101	151
Parents 3	102	102	152
Parents 4	103	103	153
Parents 5	104	104	154
Parents 6	105	105	155

The statistic known as the correlation coefficient (discussed on pages 78-80) measures the relationship between two variables, in this case, the relationship between the parents' IQ and children's IQ.

In the case of the parents and Twin 1, the correlation is perfect because, as the IQs of the parents rise, so do those of the children and in a perfectly predictable way. The two sets of IQs are perfectly correlated. The value of the correlation coefficient is +1.0. Thus we would be inclined to say that genes played a big role in the determination of the

IQs of the children known as Twin 1 because the correlation between parents' and children's IQs is so high.

What about Twin 2? The correlation between parents' IQs and the IQs of those called Twin 2 is also a perfect +1.0. To get a perfect correlation, the two numbers do not have to be identical. All that has to happen is that as one number (e.g., parent IQ) increases, the other number (child's IQ), increases in a perfectly predictable way. The measured IQ of each Twin 2 is irrelevant to the correlation coefficient. Recall that the correlation coefficient measures only the relationship between two variables. Looking at parents' IQs and at the IQs of the Twin 2s, we see that, as the parents' IQs increase, so do those of the children and in a perfectly predictable way. Once again, genes loom large.

But the IQ of each Twin 2 is, in each case, *50 points higher* than that of the parents or of Twin 1. This makes it appear that the intellectual stimulation provided by the researchers — i.e., nurture — had a huge impact. An IQ of 100 is at the 50th percentile; an IQ of 150 is above the 99th percentile.

The body of literature concerning the relative influences of nature and nurture shows that correlational research always makes genes seem important, while experimental research highlights the impact of nurture — although the effects are not nearly as large as in our theoretical study. Correlational research, naturally, uses correlation coefficients. Experimental research reports data in terms of mean differences induced by the experimental treatment. In this case, our experimental treatment induced a mean difference of 50 IQ points between parents and the second twin's.

There are a variety of tests that yield a number called IQ. Perhaps the most famous are the Stanford Binet and the Wechsler. The Wechsler was initially constructed psychologist David Wechsler at Bellevue Hospital in New York City and called the Wechsler-Bellevue. Later, two separate IQ tests

were developed from the first version, the Wechsler Adult Intelligence Scale, (WAIS, pronounced Ways) and the Wechsler Intelligence Scale for Children (WISC-R, the "R" standing for "revised" after the test was revised in 1974).

Wechsler constructed his tests in part in reaction to the Stanford Binet's emphasis on verbal skills. The Wechsler gave equal attention to "performance" tests such as completing pictures, arranging pictures, copying geometrical designs with a set of blocks, putting objects together, and solving mazes. In later years, the areas covered by the two tests have converged. For instance, the WISC-R contains a verbal scale as well as a performance scale, consisting of vocabulary, arithmetic, comprehension, the judgment of similarities, and the processing of verbal information.

Other tests in this general category include the Otis-Lennon School Ability Tests, the Woodcock-Johnson, and the Peabody Picture Vocabulary Test. The last has the advantage of being relatively fast to administer individually. Some IQ tests have also been developed to administer in group settings. The correlations among these various tests are typically quite high.

Is "IQ" Unitary?

As discussed above, American psychologists working with IQ tests operated on the assumption that IQ reflected a unitary mental process, usually referred to as *g* for general. This unitary process affected virtually everything a person did. Other psychologists, thought that there was no *g* factor, that intelligence was made up of a series of separate, independent abilities.

A theory of separate intelligences developed by Howard Gardner at Harvard has become popular in some quarters. In addition to the usual kinds of intelligence that most people think of — what Gardner dubbed verbal-linguistic and logical-mathematical — spatial intelligence is associated with artists or architects. Bodily-kinesthetic intelligence is demonstrated by dancers and athletes, and musical intelligence is exhibited by the various musical performers. A person high in intrapersonal intelligence is a person who can "get in touch with himself." People high in interpersonal intelligence can read other people and would do well as politicians or diplomats.

Since postulating the above seven intelligences in 1983, Gardner has added two more. Those gifted with naturalist intelligence can identify fauna and flora and solve problems about them. People with an abundance of existential intelligence are those who reason about life, death, and ultimate truths.

Other people have noticed talents such as musical talent, of course, but have relegated it to a sphere outside of "intelligence." They have argued, like Goddard, that intelligence is a unitary trait that influences virtually all behavior. Gardner, by contrast, elevates these talents to the same level as traditional IQ and chides schools for being so dominated by verbal-linguistic and logical-mathematical intelligences.

Gardner's identification of intelligences is not arbitrary. He establishes criteria which any talent must meet to be called a true intelligence:

1. A location in a specific area of the brain as indicated by studies of brain injury and degenerative diseases.
2. The existence of *idiots savants* and exceptional individuals. Examples include Mozart's being able to perform on the piano at age 4 (often reproducing something he had just heard played by a full orchestra) or Dustin Hoffman's character in *Rain Man*.
3. A set of core operations.
4. An identifiable set of stages of growth in an individual with "mastery level" as the end state.
5. A development that can be traced through the evolutionary history of humankind.
6. Specific tasks that reflect the intelligence.
7. A set of psychological tests that identify and quantify the intelligence.
8. A set of "images" by which the intelligence is encoded into a symbol system — languages, mathematics, musical notation, etc.

CHAPTER 6

Interpreting Test Scores

So far we have talked about test scores mostly in terms of percentile ranks, but we have other metrics to use in reporting test scores. These other metrics include grade equivalents, normal-curve equivalents, standard scores, and stanines. We discuss each of these in turn.

GRADE EQUIVALENTS

Teachers and parents love grade equivalents. They have such an intuitive appeal. If Suzy is in the third month of the third grade and gets a grade equivalent of 3.3, the teacher can tell the parents that Suzy is "at grade level," and the parents can go home thinking that Suzy is where she should be for her age (unless, of course, they think of Suzy as a superior student). But, as with a national norm, 50% of all children are by definition below "grade level."

Using grade equivalents, test makers define "grade level" as the score of the average student in a particular grade. A student in the third month of the third grade who obtains the "grade level" score, gets a grade equivalent of 3.3. Remember, by this definition, 50% of all students, nationally, are below grade level. This kind of definition leads to a lot of mischief if, for instance, newspapers have reported that 30% (or so) of the members of a graduating class in a high school are not reading at grade level (they usually pick an affluent school which enhances the sense of scandal). People who are not aware of how test publishers define grade level will assume, quite naturally, that all grad-

uating seniors should be reading at grade level and if they aren't what on earth is the district doing giving them diplomas? But, to repeat, even if all the students in Lake Wobegon are above grade level, half of all students in the nation will be below grade level — by definition.

A more common rascality often occurs when a child in, say, the fourth grade brings home a test report declaring that she is reading at seventh-grade level. Why, the parents are likely to wonder, is my child not in seventh grade, at least for her reading, since she is reading at seventh-grade level?

But she is not reading at seventh-grade level. The seventh-grade level for seventh-graders is the score that the average seventh-grader would score on seventh-grade reading material. When a fourth-grader gets a grade equivalent of 7 on a test, it represents what the average seventh-grader would score on *fourth-grade reading material.*

And actually, this might not even be true because no seventh-graders have taken the fourth-grade test. None. Zip. Zero. Test publishers cannot afford too much out-of-grade testing, such as giving the fourth-grade test to seventh-graders. Mostly, they give the fourth-grade test to some sample of third-graders and fifth-graders. The projection of how a typical seventh-grader would score is a statistical extrapolation based on the scores of third-, fourth-, and fifth-graders. We have no idea how accurate it might be beyond those grades.

Still more trouble arises when people average grade equivalents. They look like they can be averaged. After all, they're numbers, aren't they? Grade equivalents may look like any other numbers, but they are not. In science there are a variety of scales that have different mathematical properties. In ascending order of precision, these scales are called nominal, ordinal, equal interval, and equal ratio. A scale must attain the status of "equal interval" before its numbers can be meaningfully averaged.

In an "equal interval scale" the distance between one number and the next is always the same. In such a scale numbers can be averaged. Temperature, whether in degrees Celsius or Fahrenheit, is such a scale. Each degree represents the same amount of heat. Taking one temperature reading of 60° and another of 40° and calculating an average of 50° is reasonable and gives a meaningful result.

Grade equivalents do not form an equal interval scale. Averaging grade equivalents is more like averaging house numbers (an ordinal scale). You know that 608 S. Elm Street is farther south than 604 S. Elm, but 606 South Elm (the average), might be quite close to 608 and quite far away from 604. Or it might not even exist.

PERCENTILES

We have already discussed percentiles, but we should mention here that they are not an equal interval scale, either. In terms of distance along the normal curve, a gain from the 50th percentile to 60th is much smaller than a gain from 80th to 90th. This is shown opposite in Figure 2.

NORMAL-CURVE EQUIVALENTS

Researchers developed the normal-curve equivalent (NCE) in an attempt to remedy the problems discussed above concerning grade equivalents and percentile ranks. The NCE was an attempt to create an equal interval scale for testing. Instead, it just created incomprehensibility. If your child scores at the 60th percentile, you know he did better than 60% of the kids in the population tested. If he gets an NCE of 60, you could learn, by looking at the normal curve opposite, that he scored better than 68% of the other students. For a percentile rank, you don't need to look at the normal curve. But an increase of your child's NCE from 60 to 70 doesn't mean that he scored better than 78% of the students. It means he scored better than 83% of the other kids — something you could learn only by looking at the normal curve again. Well, you could memorize all of these numbers, but no one bothers when percentile ranks give them to you automatically.

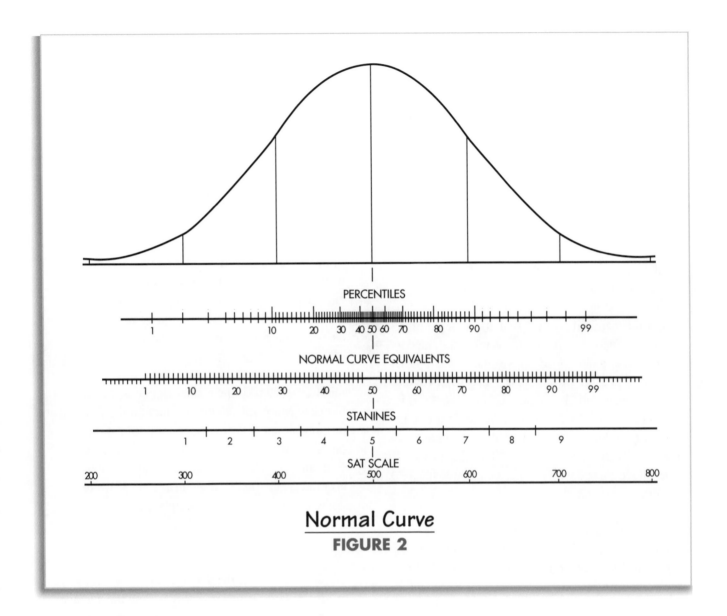

PERCENTILES

NORMAL CURVE EQUIVALENTS

STANINES

SAT SCALE

Normal Curve
FIGURE 2

It would be something else if NCEs had what psychometricians call "construct validity." If, say, an increase from an NCE of 50 to 60 meant an increase in some defined psychological trait and if an increase from 60 to 70 meant the same amount of increase, then NCEs would take on new life and form a true equal interval scale. But they don't have any construct validity, because their origins were purely statistical. They were not developed in connection with any construct, such as intelligence, ability, achievement, or anything else. All you can know about NCEs is that bigger is better.

STANDARD SCORES

Standard scores are the most technical of the various types of scores, but they are also the most familiar. An IQ score is a standard score. So is a score on the SAT, ACT, NAEP, GRE, LSAT, GMAT, TIMSS, and so forth. Almost all commercial achievement tests come with some scale referred to as a "growth scale" or "developmental scale." These, too, are standard scores. Unlike percentile ranks, which only tell you where your child stands in regard to other children, scaled scores in a growth scale can permit you to see how much progress your child has made between, say,

> People almost never use stanines any more. If you see them, be suspicious because someone might be trying to hide something.

grades three and four. School districts seldom make use of these kinds of standard scores.

All of the standard scores listed above begin life as a scale defined in terms of an average, the standard deviation, and the normal curve (the standard deviation is a measure of score variability discussed in "Some Terms and Technicalities" on page 73. It is a good idea to skip ahead and read about it now). Suppose we have a bunch of test scores whose mean is 50 and whose standard deviation is 10. The following scores have those characteristics: 20, 30, 40, 50, 60, 70, 80.

Suppose we take each of these scores, subtract the mean from it, and divide by the standard deviation. The set of sample scores would now look like this:

$$(20-50)/10 = -3$$
$$(30-50)/10 = -2$$
$$(40-50)/10 = -1$$
$$(50-50)/10 = 0$$
$$(60-50)/10 = +1$$
$$(70-50)/10 = +2$$
$$(80-50)/10 = +3$$

Our scores now range from -3 to +3. But take a look at what happened to, say, a score of 80:

$$(80-50)/10 = +3.$$

If the mean is 50 and the standard deviation is 10, then a score of 80 is 30 points — three standard deviations — above the mean. And when we subtracted the mean and divided by the standard deviation, we got a new score in terms of standard deviation units: $(80-50)/10 = +3$. The whole set of scores now looks like this: 20 becomes -3; 30 becomes -2; 40 becomes -1; 50 becomes 0; 60 becomes +1; 70 becomes +2; 80 becomes +3.

These numbers are called standard scores, often referred to as z scores (nothing magical, just a convention to call them z's). They are scores that indicate a person's position on the normal curve. Oh sure, you could know this position by keeping in mind the mean and standard deviation, but each new test would have a different mean and a different standard deviation, and the whole process of thinking about where a person is on the normal curve would become impossibly cumbersome.

And if you don't keep the standard deviation in mind for each test, the results can be misleading. Suppose Mary scored 70% correct on the first test of the year and 73% on the second. She did better on the second, right? Well, by one criterion, percent correct, yes. And if we are grading on an absolute scale, that's all we need. But if we're "grading on the curve" or simply want to know Mary's position relative to other students, we're in the dark.

We don't yet know the average scores so we can't tell if her score is better or worse than the average. Let's assume that the average was 60 on the first test and 65 on the second. Now it begins to look like, relatively speaking, she did better on the first test than on the second, scoring 10% correct above average on the first, but only 8% better than average on the second. But let us further suppose that the standard deviation was 5 on the first tests and 10 on the second. That makes Mary +2 standard deviations above the mean on the first test $(70-60)/5$. Only 2 % of the students will score higher (assuming the distribution of scores forms a bell curve). Mary scores better than the 50% below average, better than the 34% between the mean and +1 standard deviation, and better than the 14% between +1 and +2 standard deviations above the mean. These add up to 98%.

But her performance on the second test makes her only +.8 standard deviations above the mean — (73-65)/10. She scored better than 79% of the students on the second test (I know this because I looked it up in a table in a statistics book).

For all tests, though, the standard scores will always range between -3 and +3. "Plus 3" (+3) means three standard deviations above the mean. "Minus 3" (-3) means three standard deviations below. Easy to remember. Much easier than juggling all those means and standard deviations for each test.

The conversion from raw scores to z scores does not change the relationship of the scores to one another in any way. If I know that a person got a z score of +1, I know he did better than 84% of the rest of the test-takers. How do I know this? Well, 50% of the scores fall below the mean (assuming a normal distribution here so that the mean, median, and mode are all the same). So the student scored better than this group. And 34% of all scores will fall between the mean and +1 standard deviation. The student did better than this group, too. These two figures sum to 84%.

This is discussed in the technical section on the normal curve but is mostly something that needs to be memorized. Thirty-four percent of all scores will fall between the mean and +1 standard deviations, and 34% will fall between the mean and -1 standard deviation. Another 14% will fall between +1 and +2 standard deviations and between -1 and -2 standard deviations. So, in all normal curves, 96% of all scores will fall between -2 and +2 standard deviations from the mean. Check the normal curve graph on page 67 to see a visual representation of this. It would be a good idea to get familiar with some of this curve's common statistical properties.

But, you say, I just told you that IQ scores and SAT scores are standard scores, and these scores don't look anything like IQ or SAT scores. True, but we can easily get from what we have to IQ and SAT scores. Let's take each z score from -3 to +3,

multiply by 15 and add 100. A z score of 0 — the mean — becomes 0 x 15 + 100 = 100. A z score of +3 becomes 3 x 15 + 100 = 145, and so forth. The distribution of scores now looks like this: 145, 130, 115, 100, 85, 70, 55.

Voilà, an IQ distribution. It has a mean of 100 and a standard deviation of 15. It could have a mean of 50 and a standard deviation of 5 — the choice of scale is completely arbitrary.

When you multiply a set of test scores by a constant (15 in this case) or add a constant (100 in this case) to a set of test scores, you are performing what statisticians call a "linear transformation" on the numbers. Linear transformations do nothing to alter the relationship of the numbers (if you squared any of the numbers or took the square root of any or raised any to some higher power, you'd be making nonlinear transformations, and some relationships would change).

When the College Board built the SAT, it wanted a scale that could not be confused with any other set of scores. So the statisticians simply took their z scores, multiplied by 100 and added 500. A z score of 0 is the z score of the mean raw score. Then, 0 x 100 + 500 = 500, the average score on the SAT.

This exposition on standard scores is presented not because they are magical or in any way mysterious. Indeed, my purpose is just the opposite: to remove the mystery. Standard scores are used everywhere, so it is a good idea to have some notion of where they come from and how they can be interpreted — or misinterpreted.

STANINES

People almost never use stanines any more. If you see them, be suspicious because someone might be trying to hide something (unless, as with our sample test report on page 3, the stanines are only one of a number of types of scores reported).

Stanine is short for "standard nine," and its invention was an artifact of the old don't "fold, spindle, or mutilate" type of computer punch cards. As readers of a certain age will recall, these cards had 80 columns, each of which contained the numbers 0 through 9. One of these numbers would have a hole punched through it.

Space on these cards was precious. An IQ test score would take three columns (even for IQs under 100, because the space had to be reserved in case the IQ was over 100, something that couldn't be known in advance). Someone in the Air Force realized that, if test scores could be condensed into a single digit, two of these valuable columns would be freed up for other data. Each of the stanines represents a certain percentage of the normal curve as follows:

Stanine

1	2	3	4	5	6	7	8	9

Percentage

4	7	12	17	20	17	12	7	4

Thus the bottom 4% of the scores are the first stanine; the top 4%, the ninth.

Why did I say that people might be hiding something when they use stanines? It is common practice to consider the fourth, fifth, and sixth stanines, the three stanines in the middle, as "average." If you add up these three stanines, you get 54% of the scores. These can be reported as average. The seventh, eighth, and ninth stanines contain another 23% of the scores. These can be reported as "above average." So if you are an enterprising school public relations official, you can tell the media that 77% (54% + 23%) of your students are average or above average! Only the bottom 23% of the scores — those in the first, second, and third stanines — need be reported as "below average."

Let's assume your school district is perfectly "normal" and that its average score is the same as the national norm — the 50th percentile. If your district reported its test scores in percentile ranks, 50% of the students would be below average. But if the percentile ranks are collapsed into stanines, only those with a percentile rank of 23 or below would be reported as below average. Hey, this is almost as good as Lake Wobegon!

CHAPTER 7

Some Terms and Technicalities

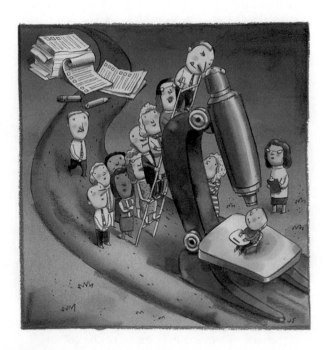

The mean is what most people think of as an "average." We all learned to calculate a mean in school. You just add up all the numbers and then divide by the number of numbers. The symbol for "to add up all of the numbers" or "to sum" is represented by the capital Greek letter sigma, Σ, while each value is represented by an x. The symbol for the mean is sometimes capital M, but more often a capital X with a horizontal bar over the top and called "X bar." In the distribution of "scores" listed below, the sum of all 11 numbers is 35,000,460,000. This sum, divided by 11, yields a mean of 3,181,860,000.

FIGURE 3
Distribution of Wealth

1. 10,000
2. 10,000
3. 20,000
4. 25,000
5. 45,000
6. 50,000
7. 55,000
8. 75,000
9. 80,000
10. 90,000
11. 35,000,000,000

$\Sigma \chi = 35,000,460,000$

$\text{M or } \overline{X} = \Sigma \chi / n = 35,000,460,000/11 = 3,181,860,000$

Sooner or later, if you hang out with test scores, you will encounter a number of terms that have precise technical meanings. I've already described a few, such as percentile rank and scaled score. This section defines and discusses more such terms. I'll try to keep this discussion in plain English, but if you have any suggestions for improvements to the descriptions, please send them along.

Let's begin by bringing forward into the body of the text the three terms that were footnoted earlier: mean, median, and mode. These terms are all a kind of average or, as statisticians say, a measure of central tendency.

The use of one value — 35 billion — so much larger than the rest is not an accident. That figure is the estimated wealth in dollars of Bill Gates, founder of Microsoft, in August 1997. (In spite of the nation's economic slowdown, as this is written in October 2001, the sum has risen to $68 billion.) The other values are arbitrary and represent the wealth of other residents of Microsoft's hometown, Redmond, Washington. For convenience, we have populated Redmond with only 10 people other than Gates.

I chose these 11 values to illustrate an important fact: the mean is affected by extreme values. And if such extremes are extreme enough or occur with some frequency, the mean will not be a meaningful measure of central tendency. In the case shown above, the "average" wealth is over three billion dollars, while, in reality, only one resident has wealth that high, and nobody else is worth even as much as a hundred thousand dollars.

Some extreme values distort things in weather reports. It seems some years are extra-hot or extra-cold or extra-wet or extra-dry. When extra-hot and extra-cold years are averaged, we get a moderate average year that never actually existed.

We can describe an average where extreme values have no impact by using the median (usually written as Mdn). By definition, half of all scores are above the median, and half are below. We have been using one median throughout this book — the 50th percentile of a distribution of test scores. The national norm of a test score distribution is a median. In the hypothetical distribution of incomes in Redmond, Washington, half of the scores fall above 50,000, and half fall below that figure, so the median is 50,000.

Since we are just counting how many people score above a point and how many people score below it, Bill Gates is just another guy — for our purposes, equal to everyone else. For the income data presented here, the median is a "better" average in that it better represents the wealth of the residents of our simplified version of Redmond.

The final way of representing an average is called the mode. It is simply the score that occurs most often. In Figure 3, the mode is 10,000, even though that value is also the lowest score in the whole distribution. Again, an average might not be a meaningful representation of the group.

Now, if a distribution of scores is "normal," that is, if the scores form a bell curve, then all three measures of average will be identical. If they are not identical, that is one way you have of telling that the distribution of scores is not normal without looking at the actual distribution. This feat (knowing whether or not scores are distributed normally) is not particularly important for parents or teachers except for this: many of the calculations used by statisticians concerning test scores presume a normal curve.

If the scores are not distributed normally, a number of calculations lose their validity, most notably the test for statistical significance, which we'll discuss shortly. In many cases it would probably be wise to graph the distribution of scores to get a visual impression of how much it deviates from a bell curve.

Whatever term is used for average, it is often misinterpreted. In the Third International Mathematics and Science Study (TIMSS), for instance, American eighth-graders got 53% of the items right, while the international average was 55%; in science the American kids got 58% correct, while the international average was 56%. Thus we finished very close to average in both subjects.

The media translated average into "mediocre" although the first is a statistic and the second a judgment. What the media failed to note was that most countries got very similar scores. The 58% correct in science put America in 19th place among the 41 countries in the study. Bulgarian students managed to get 4% more correct. This sent them soaring to fifth place. Icelandic students got 6% fewer items correct. This sent them plummeting to 30th place. Note that Bulgarian kids got only 10% more of the items correct than Icelandic students, but this makes a difference of 25 ranks (Bulgaria 5th, Iceland 30th). Thus, if America is "mediocre," the entire developed world is mediocre. Of the industrialized nations of Europe and Asia, only Finland and Taiwan did not participate in TIMSS eighth-grade assessment.

THE STANDARD DEVIATION

A law everyone learns in elementary statistics — and then immediately forgets — is "no measure of central tendency without a measure of dispersion." Means, medians, and modes — measures of central tendency — should never be used in isolation, although they usually are. And they can be misleading as this old joke about three statisticians shows. Three statisticians went deer hunting. They had not been out long when they spied a huge 12-point buck. The first statistician fired and missed by exactly 10 inches to the left. The second statistician then fired and missed by exactly 10 inches to the right. The third statistician exclaimed, "We got him!"

Measures of dispersion give some idea of how the scores are distributed around the average. The simplest measure of dispersion is the range. If the children in your child's class all score between the 23rd percentile and the 92nd percentile on a test, then the range is 69 percentile ranks (92 minus 23). We would simply say that the range is from 23 to 92.

Although it is always good to know the range of scores, the range might not be particularly useful

because, like the mean, it can be affected by extreme scores. For the Redmond income data, the range is enormous, even though most scores are tightly bunched around a much lower value. In fact, a single extreme score has more impact on the range than on the mean. Gates' wealth alone defines one end of the range, but it is only one of 11 values that go into calculating the mean.

The most common measure of dispersion is called the "standard deviation." I give the formula for those who want to know how it is calculated. Anyone else can skip this part.

$$SD = \sqrt{\frac{\Sigma (X - \bar{X})^2}{N}}$$

The important thing about the standard deviation is its relationship to the normal curve. We know, for instance, that in a normal curve, 34% of the scores lie between the mean and one standard deviation below the mean. Another 34% lie between the mean and one standard deviation above it. Between one and two standard deviations in either direction lie roughly another 14% of the scores. The standard deviation is used in the calculation of standard scores, as discussed on pages 67-68. It is also used in the calculation of statistical significance and effect sizes, which we take up in the following section. It is an indispensable statistic. No home should be without one.

STATISTICAL SIGNIFICANCE AND EFFECT SIZE

I give the concept of statistical significance its own separate section for two reasons: 1) it is the most technical concept in the booklet, and 2) it is a very important concept that is often misinterpreted.

People often interpret statistically significant results as meaning that the results have practical significance. In fact, you cannot make any judgment about practical significance from statistical significance, and that is the main reason that I have made statistical significance share this section with its less famous sidekick, effect size. To begin to make judgments of practical significance, you need to know an effect size (or something like it). While the material in this section is somewhat technical, the concepts are important. It might take a couple of times through before you begin to feel comfortable with them. Pretend you're back in school.

It is particularly important not to confuse statistical significance with educational importance. I recommend that you supplement the material you read here with a two-part series by James Shaver, "Chance and Nonsense: A Conversation About Interpreting Tests of Statistical Significance," which appeared in the September and October 1985 issues of the *Phi Delta Kappan*. Shaver presents the material in an easy-to-read format as a conversation between two teachers in the teachers' lounge.

Researchers perform tests of statistical significance for experiments involving two or more groups. Let's take the simplest case of just two groups. Figure 4 opposite shows the results of an experiment, let's say, teaching one group of first-graders to read using a whole language approach and teaching another group using a phonics approach. At the end of the year of teaching, the children were given a reading test (for the moment let's assume that the test is equally fair to both approaches in terms of what it tests). Two normal curves are generated, one each for the scores of the children taught by the two methods. The difference between the two groups is represented by the letter D or, sometimes, the Greek letter Δ (delta).

As educational practitioners, we want to know whether phonics or whole language is the better method of teaching reading. The traditional approach to answering this question is through a test of statistical significance. But statistical significance tells you nothing about the impact of a treatment, even though people almost always act as it if does.

Now, here comes the most technical concept in this treatise. You found that the two groups differed by some amount. You do some statistical calculations to see if the results are statistically significant. Here is what statistical significance tells you: *How likely is it that you would find a difference (D or Δ) between the two groups as large as you did find if the two groups really did not differ? Or, as the statisticians say, if the two samples actually came from populations with the same mean.*

The key words above are "How likely." A statement of statistical significance is a statement of likelihood, of odds, of probability. It is *not* a statement of magnitude. "How likely" is the result you found due to real differences? How likely is it that these differences occurred by chance? A statement about statistical significance is *not* a statement about the magnitude of those differences. About magnitude, statistical significance is silent.

The point bears repeating. Statistical significance speaks to odds. What were the odds of finding the results you did find if there really is no difference between the groups? If the odds that you've found a difference where there is none are small enough, the result is said to be statistically significant. Typically, results are considered significant if the statistical test for significance says that your result would happen by chance less than five times in 100. I don't think this is an adequate criterion, although most researchers use it. Personally, I don't want to build a discipline on results where I can be wrong one time in 20. I prefer the next level of significance usually reported where the odds of the result happening by chance are less than one in 100.

When researchers talk about statistical significance, they say things like "*p* less than point oh five" or "*p* less than point oh one." The first is their way of describing the first level of significance given in the paragraph above — five chances in 100 (or one

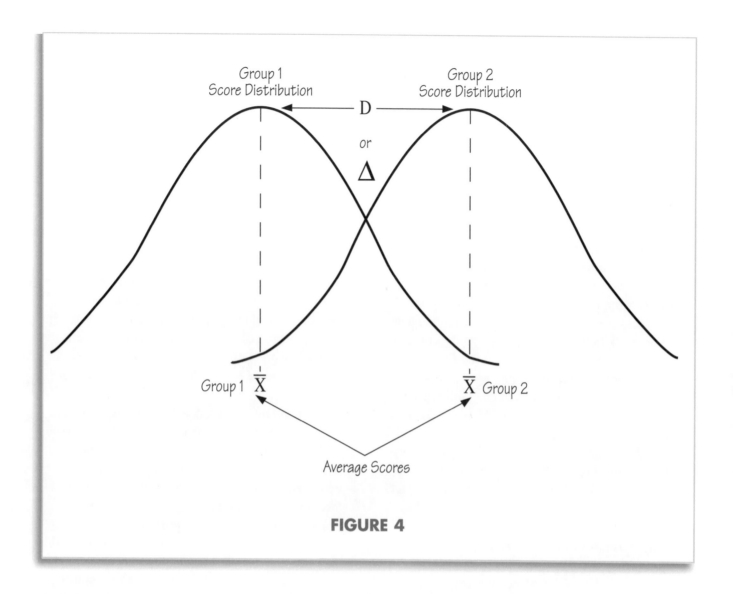

Group 1
Score Distribution

Group 2
Score Distribution

D

or

Δ

Group 1 $\overline{X}$

$\overline{X}$ Group 2

Average Scores

FIGURE 4

in 20) that the results are due to chance. The second describes the more stringent level — one chance in 100 that the results are due to chance. When they write it down, the statements of significance look like this: $p < .05$ and $p < .01$. (The letter p stands for probability of seeing the observed results by chance, and < is the mathematical symbol for "less than.")

To go back to our example, a "p less than point oh one (.01)" does not mean that whole language had more impact on beginning reading than if we found a "p less than point oh five (.05)." The p stands for probability. If you get a $p < .01$, you're not very likely to be wrong if you say there's a real difference between whole language and phonics.

If you're not familiar with statistical significance testing, you can be forgiven for wondering what all the fuss is about. You gave the tests, the two groups differed, what's the problem? Why do we even need these tests?

The problem is that you didn't test everyone or, as statisticians say, the entire population. If you gave the test to all first-graders in the country, you wouldn't have to conduct a test of significance (we'll ignore the issue of "measurement error" here and assume for the sake of this argument that our tests are perfect measures). Whatever differences you found would be real, and that would be the end of it.

But no one can afford to test all 3,000,000 or so first-graders in the U.S. So we perform our experiments on small numbers of students — on samples. And usually we use what researchers call samples of convenience: the kids in the local schools. Any time you take a sample of a population, there's a chance that your sample is not representative of the whole population.

The samples used in educational research are often quite small, perhaps only two classrooms, so the possibility that they are not representative of the nation as a whole is substantial. The chance that we have non-representative samples in our experiments is increased by the fact that most of our samples are not random samples. To have a random sample, all 3,000,000 first-graders in the country would have to have an equal chance of being chosen for the experiment. But, again, such a procedure for most research would be prohibitively expensive and impractical. You'd have to go all over the country testing kids or bring kids from all over the country to a central location. Not readily done, so most researchers use samples of convenience — the kids they can find in the neighborhood schools. The only regular testing conducted in this country that uses genuine random samples is the testing carried out by NAEP.

The notion of error introduced by sampling is not really a new notion to most people, although they might not recognize it in this context. Any time you see a Gallup or Roper or Harris poll reported, you will see a footnote to the effect that the poll has a "margin of error" of plus or minus 4% (or 3% or 5%). What this means is, "We sampled a certain number of people in our poll, and we got the results we show you. If we sample another group, the results might not be precisely the same, and this 'margin of error' gives you an estimate of how different the results could be."

Pollsters could use random samples if they wished since they are dealing with adults by telephone and only a tiny minority of people do not have a phone in the home. But they don't use random samples because they want to guarantee that their samples

have certain demographic characteristics. Pollsters have extremely sophisticated ways of sampling and can make statements about national results with samples of only about 1,000 to 1,300 well-chosen people. Educational research, alas, is not in a position to conduct such research. We are usually stuck with samples of convenience — the kids nearby.

The fact that we use samples of convenience brings up an important and often ignored aspect of educational and psychological research: studies need to be replicated. Replication is the norm in the natural sciences, but not in the behavioral sciences. When two guys in Utah claimed they had accomplished cold fusion, a process that would revolutionize energy use and bankrupt the OPEC nations (it would destroy the need for oil), laboratories all over the world swung into action to see if they could reproduce the results.

In the natural sciences, a fact is not a fact until lots of people have demonstrated it is so. But, for some reason, replication has never had this honorable status in the behavioral sciences: a replication won't count toward promotion and tenure and so people don't do replications. (Every so often, someone at a university proposes that the master's theses at that university be replications. This would have the effect of introducing the students to well-conducted research and at the same time contribute to the body of knowledge in the field. The proposal is always rejected, usually on the grounds — bogus, I would argue — that it is more important for the student to devise "original" research.

The use of an "effect size" (ES) is an attempt to transform results from statements of probability into a quantitative form that addresses, well, effect size. To take the simplest case of two groups again, suppose we instruct one group with a program designed to increase problem-solving ability and a second group, the control group, receives no such treatment. At the end of the treatment, we give a problem-solving test to both groups.

A test of statistical significance will tell us how likely we were to see whatever differences we find if the two groups really didn't differ. The calculation of the effect size will tell us how much impact the problem-solving training had, if it had any at all. To calculate an effect size, we simply subtract the mean of the control group from the mean of the experimental group and divide by the standard deviation of the control group. Here are some made up data to provide examples:

Example 1

Control Group: $\overline{X} = 50$, SD $= 10$

Experimental Group: $\overline{X} = 60$, SD $= 12$

$$ES = \frac{60 - 50}{10} = \frac{10}{10} = +1.0$$

Example 2

Control Group: $\overline{X} = 73$, SD $= 12$

Experimental Group: $\overline{X} = 70$, SD $= 14$

$$ES = \frac{70 - 73}{12} = \frac{-3}{12} = -.25$$

TABLE

What do we have here? We have one version of a standard score, which is discussed on pages 67-69. You might want to jump back and reread those pages before proceeding. The difference between an effect size and the standard scores described earlier is that the standard scores discussed elsewhere are for individuals, and these are for groups. For the sake of argument, let's say we get an effect size of +1.00. What does that mean? It means that the average score of the students who received the training in problem solving was as good as the

84th percentile of the kids in the control group. Recall that a standard score of +1 is a score one standard deviation above the mean. Fifty percent of all scores are below the mean, and another 34% are between the mean and +1 standard deviations, hence a total of 84%. We could also say that the size of the effect is the equivalent of taking a child at the 16th percentile and moving him to the 50th, or taking a child at the 84th percentile and moving him to the 98th; each of these moves is a distance of one standard deviation.

And that means the treatment was very, very powerful. A treatment that moves a child from being average to being well above average is not often seen. We don't usually get effect sizes of +1 or larger. So judging how big an effect is big enough to be of practical significance is a point of some contention among researchers. Some think that an effect size begins to take on practical importance when it's about +.25. Others are more conservative and hold out for +.35, and some even accept +.20. If you get an effect size of +.3, this is equivalent to moving a person who initially scored at the 50th percentile to the 62nd percentile. (This is something that you could know only by looking it up in a table in a statistics book.)

To take a more real-life example, African American students score about one standard deviation below white students on a variety of tests. An educational treatment that produced an effect size of +.33 for African-American students would wipe out the ethnic difference in three years.

An effect size is not the ultimate answer to our questions about practicality. Suppose your new curriculum in problem solving cost you $7,000, as a one time investment. An effect size of +.3 for this money would be one thing. Suppose, though, that the new curriculum cost $7,000 a year. Or that it cost $70,000. Would it still be a worthy investment? There is no quantitative way of making this decision. The program and its benefits must be weighed against other potential uses for the money. No statistical procedure removes the need for human judgment.

Effect sizes have another important use, although this one is more often limited to the research community. Although researchers seldom replicate a particular study, numerous researchers do work in the same general areas like mastery learning, computer-assisted instruction, etc. Their research studies don't match each other completely, and summarizing the research in a given area was difficult until effect sizes were developed. We can take the entire body of research on a given topic, though, and convert all the outcomes into effect sizes. When we do that, we can average the effect sizes to see what the whole body of research says as a single number.

For instance, one study looked at the average effect size of all the research on retaining kids in a grade for a second year. After calculating effect sizes from hundreds of studies, the researcher found that the average effect size for all the research was -.15. Retention in grade harms children. If it helped, the effect size would have been positive.

Why all this fuss over statistical significance and effect sizes? The average reader doesn't conduct experiments. But more and more, school districts and intermediate units and states do. And so, too, does the nation. The results from the Third International Mathematics and Science Study (TIMSS) were released showing the 41 countries in the study in three groups: those that were significantly above the U.S., those that were significantly below, and those that did not differ significantly from the U.S. score. The *Orange County Record* in California looked at these three groups and reported that American students finished in the next-to-last group. Of course, such a "finish" is inevitable unless American students had scored so high that no country was significantly higher or so low that no country was significantly lower. The *Orange County Record* misinterpreted what the data said.

Similarly, when the NAEP results are released, they now contain scores for several assessments of the same subject, say, reading scores for 1992, 1994, and 1998. The report will note where the gains or losses for the nation and various states are statistically significant. Virginia will no doubt have to justify in court that a student who scores 400 on its tests passes, but one who scores 399 fails. This will require discussions of scaling, measurement error, and, probably, item-response theory.

Districts, states, and nations increasingly present their findings in terms of statistical significance and effect size. Without some knowledge of these terms, you cannot decide whether the results are being properly presented. I have attended a number of school board meetings where results from testing or research were presented as statistically significant with no presentation on what this term means. This is an important omission. Researchers have a precise meaning for significance. But school board members and parents are not usually researchers. They are more likely to live in that part of the world where "significant" means "important."

THE CORRELATION COEFFICIENT

Sooner or later, mostly sooner, anyone dealing with tests is going to come in contact with correlation coefficients. When the SAT is used to predict freshman grade-point averages, the statistic used to make that prediction is the correlation coefficient. If your child takes a "spatial relations test" and the high school counselor mentions that people who score high tend to make good pilots, someone, somewhere, has correlated the test with success in flight school. When we examine the relationship between parents' IQ scores and those of their children, the statistic used is the correlation coefficient.

There are a variety of correlation coefficients, but the one most often used is officially known as the Pearson product-moment correlation coefficient. It correlates scores or the numbers assigned to any two variables (e.g., SAT scores and college freshman grade-point averages). Another coefficient sometimes seen is the rank-order correlation coefficient. It correlates ranks and is an approximation of the Pearson product-moment correlation coefficient. If you were interested, for example, in the relationship between nations' ranks on economic competitiveness and ranks on the eighth-grade mathematics scores from the Third International Mathematics and Science Study, you would use the rank-order statistic. (Incidentally, the correlation in this case is +.09, meaning there is virtually no correlation.)

Both correlation coefficients can take on values ranging from +1.00 to -1.00. A correlation of +1.00 means that two variables are perfectly correlated: as one increases, the other increases in a perfectly predictable way. A correlation of -1.00 also means a perfect correlation, but now, as one variable moves higher, the other moves lower in a perfectly predictable way. A correlation of 0.00 means that there is no correlation: given a high score on one variable, we can't make any prediction about the value of the other variable; it might be high, average, or low.

When graphed, perfect correlations are straight lines, and a zero correlation is a circle. For values in between, the graphs of correlations are ellipses. Fat ellipses show weak correlations; thin ones show strong correlations. Figure 5 below shows perfect correlations, zero correlation, and two correlations in between, one strong, one weak, and one strong but not linear correlation. If the relationship between two variables is not linear, the correlation coefficient is an inappropriate statistic.

In the section on statistical significance, our example tested to see if two groups in an experiment differed significantly. Significance tests can be applied to correlation coefficients as well. Here the significance test determines the odds of your obtaining a correlation as large as the one you did get if the real correlation between the two variables is zero.

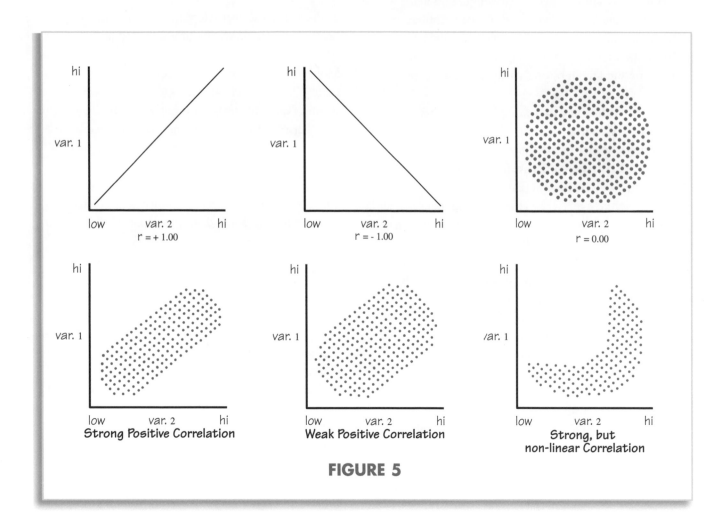

FIGURE 5

There are times when I consider forming the National Association for the Abolition of Correlation Coefficients because they cause so much misunderstanding. The reason is this: *correlation says nothing about causation.* Everyone who has even a passing acquaintance with statistics knows this. But human beings have an apparently irresistible impulse to infer causation from correlation.

In the long run, that's probably good because it allows us to notice patterns. But given a correlation between variable A and B, it might be that a variation in A causes the variation in B. It might equally be that a variation in B causes the variation in A. Or it might be that a variation in A and a variation in B are actually caused by some third variable C. Or there might not be any causal relationship between A and B at all. For example, there is a strong correlation between arm length and the length of one's shirt sleeves. But, given nothing but the correlation coefficient, it makes as much sense to say that increasing the length of sleeves will increase the length of one's arms as the reverse.

Remember this: any two variables can be correlated. That doesn't necessarily mean that the resulting correlation coefficient is meaningful. There is a correlation between who wins the Super Bowl and which political party wins the presidency. Before everyone started wearing jeans, there was a correlation between hemlines and prosperity: short hemlines meant good times; long ones indicated slowdowns. So far as I know, neither Alan Greenspan nor anyone else has ever proposed that we shorten skirts to cure our economic woes during a recession. From correlation, you cannot infer causation (but the temptation to do so seems to be hardwired in our brains.)

RELIABILITY

The essential question to ask of a test is, Is it valid? A prior question, though, is, Is it reliable? Validity is addressed in the next section.

Reliable tests give the same results each time (taking into account measurement error, also discussed below). A test that gives a different score each time a person takes it is not a reliable test (although, because of measurement error, test-takers seldom get *precisely* the same test scores). The reliability of a test is assessed with a reliability coefficient, which is nothing more or less than a correlation coefficient.

There are several reliability coefficients available. One that almost no one uses any more is test-retest reliability, the correlation between the test taken at time 1 and the same test taken again at time 2. Time 2 should be picked so that memory from time 1 doesn't influence the outcome and so that the events happening between time 1 and time 2 don't influence the results at time 2. Time 2 used to be given in textbooks as several weeks, but since no one calculates test-retest reliabilities anymore, it is not clear that this is still thought of as a standard. Indeed, as one test textbook notes, there really is no such thing as *the* test-retest coefficient because the reliability decreases with increasing time between tests.

Money is one reason no one does test-retest reliabilities. Time is also a factor. It takes twice as much of each for test-retest reliability as it does for all other reliability coefficients, which come from a single test-taking session (not counting the time in between administrations).

One option to test-retest reliability is alternative form reliability. Most testing companies develop two forms of their achievement tests, for instance, that can be used interchangeably.

Another reliability coefficient is the split-half correlation. In this case, half of the test is correlated with the other half, sometimes first half with second half, but more often odd numbered items with even numbered. Of course, if you have a 50-item test and correlate odd and even numbered items, this is the same as correlating two 25-item tests, and the result is a reliability coefficient for only a 25-item test. There is a statistical procedure for finding out what the reliability coefficient is for the entire 50-item test, which would be somewhat higher.

Finally, the most common reliability coefficients used today are variants on the split-half correlation, the Kuder-Richardson-20 (usually abbreviated to KR-20) and Cronbach's Alpha. These are based on the proportions of people passing and failing each item. The KR-20 is, mathematically, the average of all possible split-half reliabilities. This fact has some practical significance. The KR-20 should be used only when one is certain that all of the items in a test are measuring a single dimension.

To see why this is so, imagine a test with 10 vocabulary items, 10 spatial relationship items, 10 reasoning items, and 10 perceptual speed items, in that order. In doing a split-half reliability coefficient among odd and even items, you would be correlating scores on only one dimension: the five odd vocabulary items with the five even vocabulary items, the five odd spatial items with the five even and so forth. A KR-20, though, calculates all possible split-halfs. In some of these calculations, a person's scores on vocabulary items will be correlated with her scores on reasoning items and so forth. Since people differ in their relative performance on these four skills, the reliability coefficient indicated by a KR-20 will be reduced.

VALIDITY

There are various kinds of validity, too. We'll take a peek at only four: content validity, criterion validity, curriculum validity, and instructional validity. Only content validity does not presume the test has already demonstrated reliability.

Content validity simply asks the question, "Does this test measure what it claims to measure?" In the matter of school subject areas, this is not often a major issue. In some other arenas, though, the test questions come at the topic of their test somewhat obliquely. Even in school matters, though, a test can lack content validity. If a test of mathematics that used nothing but set theory were imposed on students who had learned mathematics in some other way, we wouldn't think that the test was a good measure of their achievements. A test of world history that asked questions only about events in Europe would lack content validity.

Criterion validity, also called predictive validity, calculates the correlation between performance on the test and performance on some criterion. In the case of the SAT, the criterion is freshman college grade-point average. The SAT is supposed to predict grades, and, if it doesn't, it doesn't have criterion validity.

A test is said to have curriculum validity if the content measured by the test is present in the curriculum used by the school. It has instructional validity if the content of the test is actually taught. These concepts emerged from a court case challenging a state's use of a test to qualify students for high school graduation. Plaintiffs challenged the test on the grounds that some children had not had any opportunity to learn the material the test covered. The courts ruled that the state could use the test, but only after some years during which the state had to establish that the material on the test had actually been taught. It is worth mentioning in passing that the judges in the case used the phrase, curriculum validity, but when one reads their brief, one sees quickly that they are in fact talking about instructional validity.

I said earlier that a test must be reliable before it can be valid. There are some areas of performance assessment, however, where some would argue, me included, that validity is possible in the absence of reliability. To cite an actual case: I once submitted an article to a journal that then sent the article to four reviewers who advised the editor on its fate. The reviewers used a form with four categories: "publish as is," "publish with minor changes," "publish with major changes," and "reject."

Each judge picked a different category. At one level, one would say that the "test" is unreliable since the judges couldn't agree and we should scrap the peer-review process of deciding what gets into our professional journals. Some people actually claim this. Reading the judgments, though, it was clear that the reviewers gave the paper different ratings because they held different perspectives on what was being said (reviews are done anonymously and so can be shared with authors without jeopardizing relations between reviewers and authors). Each judgment was valid from its perspective.

Outside of fields that aspire to be scientific, one sees many instances in which the "validity" of a "test," like beauty, actually comes to rest in the beholder. Consider these excepts from two reviews:

> This gripping scene in Stanley Kubrick and Arthur C. Clarke's visual masterpiece [*2001: A Space Odyssey*], not to mention more than two hours of other such moments, is yours for the taking right now. . . . I had the best movie experience this year since watching *Memento.* — Desson Howe, *Washington Post,* Weekend Section, November 2, 2001

> What a ridiculous movie! Has any film veered more toward kitsch than Stanley Kubrick's *2001: A Space Odyssey* of 1968? Now, seen in actual 2001, it's less a visionary masterpiece than a crackpot Looney Tune, pretentious, abysmally slow, amateurishly acted, and, above all, wrong. — Stephen Hunter, *Washington Post,* Style section, November 2, 2001

How do you like these two quotes as evidence for a constructivist theory of cognition? In such cases, the readers must develop a sense of validity based on whose judgments they come to trust (or not).

These kinds of differences, although not so severe, show up in some school assessments as when different teachers give different grades to the same portfolio or oral presentation. What is important is to have some person make an informed, final decision. In the case of my papers, an editor could review all reviews and render a judgment. In the case of portfolios, some teacher can act as the editor.

THE STANDARD ERROR OF MEASUREMENT
This is a technical term we will deal with only conceptually, not bothering with the formula. It would be nice if tests were perfectly accurate, but

they aren't. There is some amount of error associated with them, and it is called measurement error. The usual statistical procedure for calculating the amount of error is to compute the standard error of measurement, a straightforward procedure using other statistics concerning the test. The standard error of measurement is a variety of standard deviation.

The importance of the standard error of measurement is this: if it is large, important decisions using the test's results probably shouldn't be made. In plain English, the test isn't accurate enough. Suppose we have a test score for a person. That is called, simply enough, the observed score. In theory, the observed score might or might not be what is called the true score. We can then use the standard error of measurement to ask, "Given this observed score and this standard error of measurement, what is the range of scores within which we can be pretty certain the true score lies? For instance, given an observed score of 70 and a standard error of 2, we can be pretty certain that the person's true score is between 66 and 74 (plus or minus two standard errors).

Measurement error can have large practical ramifications. In the court case mentioned earlier, a school district wanted to retain children who did not score at a particular level. However, the standard error of measurement of the test was large enough that a child who scored one point below the passing score for third grade could actually have a true score that would be above the passing score not only for grade 3 but grades 4, 5, and 6!

In another instance, when a passing score was set for the National Teachers' Examination (NTE), a cut score or passing score was determined. Given the fact that there is some measurement error on the NTE, as on all tests, the passing score was then moved one standard error below the original cut score. This meant that most, although not all, test-takers who had true scores above the passing score would not fail the test just because of measurement error.

CHAPTER 8

Conclusion

I would hope that by the time you reach this point, you have a better idea than when you began this book of how tests are made, of what they can and can't do, and of how to interpret the results from them. I hope as much that you have acquired some "feel" for how tests can be abused by authorities. The technicalities of tests have been covered in brief. Anyone interested in pursuing them further might wish to peruse Lee Cronbach's *Essentials of Psychological Testing* (Harper & Row) or Anne Anastasi's *Psychological Testing* (Macmillan).

It is not likely that we will reduce our overreliance on tests any time soon. Although President Bush's proposal for testing all children in grades 3-8 met, at best, a lukewarm reception in the statehouses around the country, it is not because the governors are anti-test. It is in part because the states have spent money for their own, often customized, testing programs and because the President's proposal made no sense. Unfortunately, neither house of Congress realized this until after the legislation had been passed. So much for due deliberation in the legislative process. The best we can hope for is that you can use the knowledge gained from this book to keep the tests imposed on our children in their proper perspective.

APPENDIX 1

Comments on the Test Report

As promised in the first chapter, here are my comments on the CTBS Terra Nova test score report.

This is a class report that a teacher would see, but a similar report for individual children would be sent to parents describing the results for their child. In the past few years, parents have begun to demand to see not only the results but the tests. Different school systems and different states are all over the board about this. I predict that eventually parents in all states will be entitled to see the test.

Seeing the test is important for the Terra Nova (and other tests) because one can't tell from the name of the test exactly what is being tested or how. While "math computation" is straightforward, the Terra Nova also tests something called "math." What is that? There are also different tests and different formats for skills that the Terra Nova calls "language mechanics" or "language expression."

The results give a full array of test scores and ranks and define each of them. The variety of metrics allows you to choose whichever metric you feel most comfortable with — none of these scores is going to contradict another in terms of how the child performed.

The Class Record says that the class is at "grade 3.7." This means that the students were tested in the seventh month of the third grade. A grade equivalent of 3.7 would be "at grade level."

STUDENT 1

Student 1 has a wide range of scores, but not exceptionally so, especially among children of this age. Independent of whether or not Gardner's theory of multiple intelligences is right, students do not perform uniformly on all tests. Nor do they perform uniformly over time. When I analyzed test score stability, I found that typically students will show a variation of 25 percentile ranks over a four-year period. Only those below the 10th percentile and those whose ranks were in the high 90s did not.

The discrepancy between reading (65th percentile) and vocabulary (44th percentile) is probably large enough to ask the teacher about. As is the difference between "math" and math computation. The student could be having trouble with arithmetical operations, or it could be that the teacher or school does not emphasize rote computational skills.

These differences are also worth looking at because the NCEs of the two tests differ from the AANCE: the anticipated normal-curve equivalent. As with most achievement test batteries, the Terra Nova comes with an "ability" test, in this case the Test of Cognitive Skills (TCS). Scores on the TCS are used to predict how the student should do on the achievement test. Well, it's not really a prediction since all tests are taken at the same time. It reflects the misconception, discussed in the text, that an "ability" test measures "potential" while an achievement test measures how well the child is living up to that "potential."

STUDENT 2

Student 2 has an almost unbroken string of scores above the 90th percentile. Only the vocabulary test is lower, and that could easily be a chance occurrence. The 99th percentile on language mechanics has a notation to the effect that it is the highest score. This is informative because some lower scores would also be the 99th percentile. This is perhaps better seen in a longer test, such as the SAT. An 800 is a perfect score and, naturally, the 99th percentile. But the 99th percentile is made up of the top 1% of all scorers. Those who score 750, 760, 770, 780, and 790 also land in that top 1%.

The grade equivalents for this student are mostly not meaningful for reasons discussed in the text. The grade equivalent of 11.6 for reading doesn't mean that she reads as well as a second-term high school junior. Trust me on this.

STUDENT 3

Student 3 shows a contrasting pattern from extremely high to a little below average. Given that the lower scores, while mostly above average, are all in the language areas, one might wonder if this student speaks English as a native language. The subtleties of the "distractors" in language areas can throw off non-native speakers more readily than those who grew up speaking English. Even students who appear fluent in spoken English might lack the subtle skills needed to choose well among the "distractors."

Note that none of Student 3's high scores are predicted from the "ability" test. I do not know what the TCS actually measures, but however the scores are combined to make predictions, one sees a much flatter range of predicted scores than actual scores. The NCEs have a 53-point range, while the predicted range is only seven NCEs. This would appear to limit whatever utility the TCS might have.

Each student also receives a "Cognitive Skills Index" or CSI. This is some combination of scores from the TCS and is no doubt scaled to look like an IQ scale with a mean of 100 and a standard deviation of 15. Each child gets a precise score and a range of possible scores. For instance, Student 3 received a CSI of 119 with a range of 112 to 126. This no doubt takes into account plus or minus two standard errors of measurement from the actual score of 119. A student would fall into this range 96% of the time.

Note that for Student 1, the predicted AANCE is consistently larger than the observed NCE, and for Student 2 the reverse holds. This might or might not indicate something about how hard the two students are working in school, but one should resist the terms "underachiever" in the first instance or "overachiever" in the second.

Some Indicators of Achievement and School Quality Other Than Test Scores

What follows are a few things people might want to think about in addition to test scores. Some of these indicators are double-edged swords. For instance, the percentage of students taking Advanced Placement tests will depend in part on how the school wants the results to be used. Letting in only the top kids will result in smaller percentages, but higher scores to show the board and the newspapers. Letting in many more students results in higher percentages and, probably, lower scores. On the other hand, many people think that the challenge a student experiences from simply taking an Advanced Placement class is itself a rewarding experience.

Similarly, promotion and retention rates are mirror images and will differ depending on the philosophy controlling the classroom, school, or district. Most research indicates that retention is bad for kids, but high promotion rates can lead to charges of "social promotion."

Some indicators are sources of controversy. If you don't think that the state mandates for achievement are meaningful, then the percentage of students meeting these mandates won't seem important.

Finally, some indicators might not be relevant in some instances, such as percentage of students going on to college. There are places in the United States where colleges are scarce and the need for college-educated workers is low. It would be unfair to compare such places to college towns.

With that, some indicators.

Student-Based Indicators
- Percentage of Students Taking College Admission Tests
- Percentage of Students Taking Advanced Placement Courses/Tests
- Percentage of Students Going on to College and Other Postsecondary Education
- Percentage of Students Meeting State Mandates
- Dropout and Completion Rates
- Promotion and Retention Rates

Teacher-Based Indicators
- Percentage of Teachers with Majors or Minors in Teaching Area
- Percentage of Teachers Attaining Regular Certification (as opposed to emergency certification)
- Percentage of Teachers Certified by the National Board for Professional Teaching Standards
- Teacher Experience (can be a curvilinear indicator with performance lower for novices and soon-to-retire veterans)

Parent- and Community-Based Indicators
- Parent Involvement (sometimes tricky to define)
- Level of "Consumer" Satisfaction with Graduates (how universities, community colleges, employers, and the military feel about them)

Curriculum- and Equipment-Based Indicators

- Average Age of Textbooks
- Adequacy of Laboratory and Field Equipment
- Adequacy of Information Technology (involves matching the capabilities of the technologies with uses the school intends to make of them)

Other Indicators

- Programs to Develop the Qualities Tests Don't Measure (see p. iii)
- Engagement of School with External Organizations (universities, libraries, fine and performing arts groups, etc.)
- Innovative Projects
- Class Size
- Per-Pupil Expenditures

The last two indicators are controversial. Some argue that reducing class size is not cost-effective. Others say that "throwing money" at schools is ineffective. I deal with the controversies in Chapter 3 of *The War Against America's Public Schools,* concluding that while class-size reduction per se and spending per se do not increase achievement, they promote changes in practice that do. Money might not put men on the moon, but it greatly facilitates the effort.

Opportunity-to-Learn Indicators (Context of Achievement)

Schools do not exist in a vacuum. They are part of a larger community and culture, and their students are influenced by both. Indeed, from birth to age 16, children spend only 9% of their lives in schools. While school is no doubt more intense and focused than life outside of school, the outside culture exerts powerful forces. Here are some of these contextual variables.

- Teenage Pregnancy Rates and Participation in Parenting Courses
- Percentage of Female-Headed Households
- Poverty Rate
- Unemployment Rate
- Student Mobility Rate
- Paternal and Maternal Education Levels

- Percentage of Students not Speaking English as a Native Language
- Number of Violent Incidents Per Year
- Number of Annual Police Visits/Disciplinary Actions
- Physical Condition of Schools
- Demographic Trends (For example, did a corporate headquarters move into or out of the district?)

APPENDIX 3

AERA Position Statement Concerning High-Stakes Testing in Pre K-12 Education

The American Educational Research Association (AERA) is the nation's largest professional organization devoted to the scientific study of education. The AERA seeks to promote educational policies and practices that credible scientific research has shown to be beneficial and to discourage those found to have negative effects. From time to time, the AERA issues statements setting forth its research-based position on educational issues of public concern. One such current issue is the increasing use of high-stakes tests as instruments of educational policy.

This position statement on high-stakes testing is based on the 1999 *Standards for Educational and Psychological Testing*. The *Standards* represent a professional consensus concerning sound and appropriate test use in education and psychology. They are sponsored and endorsed by the AERA together with the American Psychological Association (APA) and the National Council on Measurement in Education (NCME). This statement is intended as a guide and a caution to policy makers, testing professionals, and test users involved in high-stakes testing programs. However, the *Standards* remain the most comprehensive and authoritative statement by the AERA concerning appropriate test use and interpretation.

Many states and school districts mandate testing programs to gather data about student achievement over time and to hold schools and students

accountable. Certain uses of achievement test results are termed "high stakes" if they carry serious consequences for students or for educators. Schools may be judged according to the school-wide average scores of their students. High schoolwide scores may bring public praise or financial rewards; low scores may bring public embarrassment or heavy sanctions. For individual students, high scores may bring a special diploma attesting to exceptional academic accomplishment; low scores may result in students being held back in grade or denied a high school diploma.

These various high-stakes testing applications are enacted by policy makers with the intention of improving education. For example, it is hoped that setting high standards of achievement will inspire greater effort on the part of students, teachers, and educational administrators. Reporting of test results may also be beneficial in directing public attention to gross achievement disparities among schools or among student groups. However, if high-stakes testing programs are implemented in circumstances where educational resources are inadequate or where tests lack sufficient reliability and validity for their intended purposes, there is potential for serious harm. Policy makers and the public may be misled by spurious test score increases unrelated to any fundamental educational improvement; students may be placed at increased risk of educational failure and dropping out; teachers may be blamed or punished for inequitable resources over which they have no control; and curriculum and instruction may be severely distorted if high test scores per se, rather than learning, become the overriding goal of classroom instruction.

This statement sets forth a set of conditions essential to sound implementation of high-stakes educational testing programs. It is the position of the AERA that every high-stakes achievement testing program in education should meet all of the following conditions:

Protection Against High-Stakes Decisions Based on a Single Test

Decisions that affect individual students' life chances or educational opportunities should not be made on the basis of test scores alone. Other relevant information should be taken into account to enhance the overall validity of such decisions. As a minimum assurance of fairness, when tests are used as part of making high-stakes decisions for individual students such as promotion to the next grade or high school graduation, students must be afforded multiple opportunities to pass the test. More importantly, when there is credible evidence that a test score may not adequately reflect a student's true proficiency, alternative acceptable means should be provided by which to demonstrate attainment of the tested standards.

Adequate Resources and Opportunity to Learn

When content standards and associated tests are introduced as a reform to change and thereby improve current practice, opportunities to access appropriate materials and retraining consistent with the intended changes should be provided before schools, teachers, or students are sanctioned for failing to meet the new standards. In particular, when testing is used for individual student accountability or certification, students must have had a meaningful opportunity to learn the tested content and cognitive processes. Thus, it must be shown that the tested content has been incorporated into the curriculum, materials, and instruction students are provided before high-stakes consequences are imposed for failing examination.

Validation for Each Separate Intended Use

Tests valid for one use may be invalid for another. Each separate use of a high-stakes test, for individual certification, for school evaluation, for curricular improvement, for increasing student motivation, or for other uses, requires a separate evaluation of the strengths and limitations of both the testing program and the test itself.

Full Disclosure of Likely Negative Consequences of High-Stakes Testing Programs

Where credible scientific evidence suggests that a given type of testing program is likely to have negative side effects, test developers and users should make a serious effort to explain these possible effects to policy makers.

Alignment Between the Test and the Curriculum

Both the content of the test and the cognitive processes engaged in taking the test should adequately represent the curriculum. High-stakes tests should not be limited to that portion of the relevant curriculum that is easiest to measure. When testing is for school accountability or to influence the curriculum, the test should be aligned with the curriculum as set forth in standards documents representing intended goals of instruction. Because high-stakes testing inevitably creates incentives for inappropriate methods of test preparation, multiple test forms should be used or new test forms should be introduced on a regular basis, to avoid a narrowing of the curriculum toward just the content sampled on a particular form.

Validity of Passing Scores and Achievement Levels

When testing programs use specific scores to determine "passing" or to define reporting categories like "proficient," the validity of these specific scores must be established in addition to demonstrating the representativeness of the test content. To begin with, the purpose and meaning of passing scores or achievement levels must be clearly stated. There is often confusion, for example, among minimum competency levels (traditionally required for grade-to-grade promotion), grade level (traditionally defined as a range of scores around the national average on standardized tests), and "world-class" standards (set at the top of the distribution, anywhere from the 70th to the 99th percentile). Once the purpose is clearly established, sound and appropriate procedures must be followed in setting passing scores or proficiency levels. Finally, validity evidence must be gathered and reported, consistent with the stated purpose.

Opportunities for Meaningful Remediation for Examinees Who Fail High-Stakes Tests

Examinees who fail a high-stakes test should be provided meaningful opportunities for remediation. Remediation should focus on the knowledge and skills the test is intended to address, not just the test performance itself. There should be sufficient time before retaking the test to assure that students have time to remedy any weaknesses discovered.

Appropriate Attention to Language Differences Among Examinees

If a student lacks mastery of the language in which a test is given, then that test becomes, in part, a test of language proficiency. Unless a primary purpose of a test is to evaluate language proficiency, it should not be used with students who cannot understand the instructions or the language of the test itself. If English language learners are tested in English, their performance should be interpreted in the light of their language proficiency. Special accommodations for English language learners may be necessary to obtain valid scores.

Appropriate Attention to Students with Disabilities

In testing individuals with disabilities, steps should be taken to ensure that the test score inferences accurately reflect the intended construct rather than any disabilities and their associated characteristics extraneous to the intent of the measurement.

Careful Adherence to Explicit Rules for Determining Which Students Are to Be Tested

When schools, districts, or other administrative units are compared to one another or when changes in scores are tracked over time, there must be explicit policies specifying which students are to be tested and under what circumstances students may be exempted from testing. Such policies must be uniformly enforced to assure the validity of score comparisons. In addition, reporting of test score results should accurately portray the percentage of students exempted.

Sufficient Reliability for Each Intended Use

Reliability refers to the accuracy or precision of test scores. It must be shown that scores reported for individuals or for schools are sufficiently accurate to support each intended interpretation. Accuracy should be examined for the scores actually used. For example, information about the reliability of raw scores may not adequately describe the accuracy of percentiles; information about the reliability of school means may be insufficient if scores for subgroups are also used in reaching decisions about schools.

Ongoing Evaluation of Intended and Unintended Effects of High-Stakes Testing

With any high-stakes testing program, ongoing evaluation of both intended and unintended consequences is essential. In most cases, the governmental body that mandates the test should also provide resources for a continuing program of research and for dissemination of research findings concerning both the positive and the negative effects of the testing program.

Adopted July 2000

APPENDIX 4

The Numbers Game

As promised earlier, here is my review of Nicholas Lemann's book. It appeared in the October 17, 1999 edition of the *Washington Post*.

The Big Test: The Secret History of the American Meritocracy
By Nicholas Lemann
Farrar Straus Giroux. 406 pp. $27
Reviewed by Gerald W. Bracey

What is it about the Educational Testing Service and the Scholastic Aptitude Test that generates such awe, hyperbole and hatred? First came Allan Nairn and Ralph Nader in 1980, with *The Reign of ETS: The Corporation That Makes Up Minds*. Then came David Owen in 1985, with *None of the Above: How the Educational Testing Service Controls the Gates to Higher Education and Success in American Society*. Nairn and Nader made ETS sound like the CIA, and Owen's picture looked like a cross between Big Brother and the Wizard of Oz. The University of Delaware's James Crouse and Dale Trusheim, in *The Case Against the SAT* (1988), clenched their teeth and tried to let cool statistical formulas rather than overheated rhetoric prove that the SAT doesn't help colleges select applicants, doesn't help applicants select colleges, and hurts minorities and poor kids. Now Nicholas Lemann, a national correspondent for the *Atlantic Monthly*, takes up the cudgels with *The Big Test: The Secret History of the American Meritocracy*. His treatment is the grandest in scope, the most literate and most readable. In the end, though, it is too glib and wrong — dishonest even.

It is wrong because Lemann falls into the same errors as his predecessors. While he makes fewer moral judgments about ETS, he paints the SAT as destiny itself, calling it "the all-powerful bringer of individual destiny in the United States." In his view, selective colleges established SAT-uber-alles admissions policies that led to the creation of a new class he calls "Mandarins."

Lemann presents a history in three parts. Part one describes the events leading up to the SAT, the later founding of ETS and the early years of ETS's successes. The second begins weaving in related events and following the lives of some of the newly ordained meritocrats, the Mandarins. The third focuses on these lives and their interplay, and on the roles they played in the events leading up to the defeat of affirmative action in California. It is a swaggering good tale peopled with colorful characters, from the testmakers who created the SAT in the 1920s to the students who used it 40 years later to launch themselves as Lemann's Mandarins.

The account by Lemann (Harvard '76, he refuses to divulge his SAT scores) identifies the SAT as part of a grand scheme by Harvard president James Bryant Conant and ETS's first president, Henry Chauncey, a former Harvard assistant dean, to establish a "natural aristocracy." The aristoi would be chosen on worth. IQ initially defined worth until the SAT replaced IQ tests for determining it (this replacement is more cosmetic than conceptual: The SAT correlates very highly with IQ tests). The phrase "natural aristocracy" had appeared in Thomas Jefferson's 1782 plan for public education for Virginia, and again in 1813 in a letter to John Adams, where Conant had first seen and been inspired by it. Jefferson contrasted his natural aristocracy, determined by selecting and educating people "of worth and genius," with the degenerate blood-based aristocracy in Europe.

If this sounds too ambitious, conspiratorial even, in the 1930s it was not. The early psychometricians, as testing people call themselves, knew some things. They knew that science was as deserving of their worship as any religion could ever be. They knew they were doing for psychology what Newton had done for physics: laying down the fundamental laws of the mental universe and leaving it to others to work out the details (they apparently were unaware that Newton's universe was collapsing under Einstein's assault). They knew they were right. They knew intelligence was controlled by a single gene and affected virtually everything a person tried to do in life. They knew that the "Nordic" race had more intelligence than Jews, Catholics, Greeks, Hungarians, Italians, Russians, Turks and, especially, blacks. They knew this last because Carl Campbell Brigham, the principal developer of the SAT in 1926, had reached these conclusions in his 1923 book *A Study of American Intelligence*. Brigham later recanted this view and also called the SAT a "mere supplement" to the rest of the high school record. (According to Lemann, he also opposed the establishment of ETS on the grounds that a single organization could not simultaneously conduct disinterested research in testing and promote its own products. He was right.)

Given everything that these men "knew," it is easy to appreciate their enthusiasm for grand social engineering projects, including those involving eugenics.

The book's central thesis is that Conant and Chauncey succeeded but that the whole scheme backfired. The SAT became the all-powerful determinant of admissions to selective colleges, but it tests too narrow a range of talents. Moreover, those

chosen few, blessed by the test, did not enter public service as Plato's Guardians would have but followed their own interests, particularly in the professions.

Does the case hold up? Ultimately, no, although popular culture certainly believes so. David Owen observed that "a low grade in a course is just one teacher's judgment, but a low SAT score is a brand for the ages. People who forget their shoe size don't forget what they got on the SAT" (I remember mine from 42 years ago). Some friendships dissolve on the discovery of disparate scores. And a recent *Cincinnati Post* cartoon depicted a mother reading to her child in bed: "And the little pig with the higher math and verbal lived happily ever after. The other two were swallowed by the wolf."

The thesis of the super-powerful SAT fails, though, just where it is held to be omnipotent: in the admissions offices of selective colleges. Consider admissions at Brown University, one of the most selective in the country. In 1998, Brown could have admitted all of its freshman class from applicants with SAT verbal scores above 750 (the 99th percentile) and still have had enough applicants left over to fill another whole class. The range of verbal scores that Brown actually admitted, though, was 450 points, as was the range of those who actually showed up, from 350 to 800 (for math the range was 450-800).

Brown admissions officers were engaged in a round of what Peter Moll called *Playing the Private College Admissions Game*. Dean of admissions at Vassar when he wrote his book, Moll contended that private schools admit by category. Yes, they want brains. But they want the well-rounded all-American kid, the special talent, the legacies (children of alumni) and kids with a social conscience (perhaps soon to be an endangered species). They also want, I would add, the paying guest — students who can attend without financial aid.

Colleges play the admissions game because of the vagaries of the SAT itself, something Lemann does not consider. Students' scores vary if they take the test more than once. ETS would not reveal the current score difference at which its computer suspects cheating, but David Owen put the number at 250 points (for the total). Moreover, the SAT succeeds only modestly even at its stated goal, predicting freshman grades. Correlations between the SAT and those grades generally run around .45, meaning only 20 percent (the square of the correlation) of the grades is accounted for by the test. Fully 80 percent of grades are determined by other facts.

By making the SAT the "all-powerful bringer of individual destiny," Lemann makes life itself an afterthought: "Their [the meritocracy makers'] goal was to construct a competitive race that would begin in elementary school and be substantially over by the time one graduated from college or professional school. . . . Those who like to think of American life as a great race should think of the race as beginning, not ending, when school has been completed."

As if winning cases didn't count in law firms. As if research and publications didn't count in academia. As if the most ham-fisted person could become a neurosurgeon. As if landing the big account didn't matter in corporations. In an Atlantic article on the SAT, Lemann wrote, "Today the academically selected elite does not control America to nearly the extent that is commonly assumed. Business, either corporate or entrepreneurial, isn't really its territory, and neither is career government service or elective politics." To write this and then give the SAT destiny-determining powers in his book is dishonest.

But if the Mandarins are missing from large segments of American society (and the presence of poor-boy-to-president Bill Clinton suggests that in fact they're not), how can Lemann claim that the SAT determines "the structure of success in America"? And surely some of those in corporate headquarters had high SAT scores. And if that is true, then personal characteristics, not test scores, determine where people end up. Finally, in this line

of thought, Alan Bakke, whose reverse discrimination suit against the University of California plays a pivotal role in the book, was fully 38 years old when he decided to stop being an engineer and go to medical school. If the race had been over, Bakke couldn't have gotten back on the track. Bakke is exceptional only because of his suit. Europeans are stunned by what they call the "second chance" quality of American education.

In fact, if we limit ourselves to the crass criterion of money, most research finds that going to a selective college matters some, but not a lot. The most recent, best controlled research indicates it doesn't matter at all. Researchers examined the incomes of people who were admitted to selective colleges and went, and people who were admitted but attended less selective colleges. For large samples who entered college in 1951, 1976 and 1989, there were no differences in income for the two groups.

Having said that the SAT has not created the dire problems Lemann thinks it has, let me say that it has created some problems. It creates problems when SAT-prep classes pass as high school English courses. It creates problems because poor students and minorities do not do as well as middle-class and affluent students, something ETS is apparently trying to remedy in part with its new, sure to be controversial "Strivers" program. This program is designed to reward disadvantaged students who do better than "predicted" on the SAT.

What few seem to realize is the SAT is not needed by the highly selective colleges that are supposed to make most use of it (the overwhelming majority of colleges in this country are not very selective). Some years ago, Bates and Bowdoin Colleges made the SAT an optional part of the application package but required it for students after admission — for placement and guidance purposes. Students who did not submit SAT scores with their applications scored about 150 total points lower than those who did, but they made just as good grades and did not drop out more because of academic problems.

In addition, the geographic and ethnic makeup of the schools increased as did the variety of intended majors. The faculty was happier with the class composition. There is a message in this, I think.

It is clear that Lemann has not given a lot of thought to the questions raised by his proposals or to alternatives to the SAT. Nor has he actually looked at a lot of test-related data. *The Big Test* presents a fascinating history of the development of the SAT and ETS. But its claims for the consequences of this history do not hold up when measured against the facts.

Annotated List of Resources

BOOKS

Bracey, Gerald W. (2000). *Bail Me Out! Handling Difficult Data and Tough Questions About Public Schools.* Thousand Oaks, Calif.: Corwin Press.

Provides descriptions of the non-test indicators of achievement listed. Also provides a summary of the condition of public education in the United States (insofar as that can be captured with test scores) and a guide on how to know when people are trying to use data to lie to you.

Bracey, Gerald W. (2001). *The War Against America's Public Schools.* Boston: Allyn & Bacon.

Although not specific to tests, the book shows how test results are being used to destroy the public education system and to promote vouchers and the private management of public schools.

Cookson, Peter W., Jr., and Joshua Halberstam, (1998). *A Parent's Guide to Standardized Tests in School.* New York: Learning Express.

This book provides many sample items from specific tests and general information on how to improve test scores without coaching (e.g., how to cut down on television). It gives parents practical information on coping with the school system. It is less consistent in technical areas. It mentions only one kind of validity and gives an inaccurate definition of "ability" tests.

Hanson, F. Allan (1993). *Testing Testing: Social Consequences of the Examined Life.* Berkeley, Calif.: University of California Press.

Hanson deals with tests in general — early tests for witches, lie detector tests, drug tests, pregnancy tests — as well as academic tests. Not a pretty picture overall.

Heubert, J. P., and Robert Hauser, editors (1999). *High Stakes: Testing for Tracking, Promotion, and Graduation.* Washington, D.C.: National Academy Press.

This is the report of the Committee on Appropriate Test Use convened by the National Research Council after Bill Clinton's proposal for a voluntary national test. It presumes that tests will be used for the purposes in the title and tries to determine how to minimize the potential harms from such testing. Although the committee consisted mostly of people from the testing profession, the book does not dodge tough questions.

Kohn, Alfie (2000). *The Case Against Standardized Testing: Raising the Scores, Ruining the Schools.* Portsmouth, N.H.: Heinemann.

The title says it all. Presented in a readable, informative Q and A format.

National Research Council (2001). *Knowing What Children Know: The Science and Design of Educational Assessment.* Washington, D.C.: National Academy Press.

Ohanian, Susan (2001;1999). *Caught in the Middle: Nonstandard Kids and a Killing Curriculum*; and *One Size Fits Few: The Folly of Educational Standards.* Portsmouth, N.H.: Heinemann.

Biting, angry, funny, and sad, ex-teacher Ohanian presents the case for looking at kids as individual human beings, not test scores.

Orfield, Gary, and Mindy L. Kornhaber, editors (2001). *Raising Standards or Raising Barriers? Inequality and High-Stakes Testing in Public Education.* New York: The Century Foundation.

Looks at how high-stakes tests affect poor, minority, and limited-English students.

Sacks, Peter (1999). *Standardized Minds: The High Price of America's Testing Culture and What We Can Do to Change It.* Cambridge, Mass.: Perseus Books.

In a history-oriented book, Sacks traces the rise of testing and its hurtful consequences. As one might expect from a journalist, Sacks uses many concrete, real-life examples to illustrate general conclusions. Chapter titles such as "Crusade: The Rise of Test-Driven Accountability in Our Schools" and "Beyond the SAT: Merit That Matters" give the flavor of the text.

Wiggins, Grant P. (1993). *Assessing Student Performance.* San Francisco: Jossey-Bass.

Wiggins presents a powerful and elegantly written case for performance assessment and a unique vision of testing with such surprising chapter titles as "Assessment and the Liberal Arts," "Testing and Tact," and "The Morality of Test Security."

VIDEOS

Annenberg/PBS Math and Science Collection. *Minds of Our Own.*

A three-part video series — "Can We Believe Our Eyes," "Lessons from Thin Air," and "Under Construction." Makes a powerful case for performance assessment, showing that lecturing and paper-and-pencil tests preclude teachers from knowing if students have really understood the material. Available at www.learner.org or P.O. Box 2345, South Burlington, VT 05407-2345.

WEBSITE

"None of the Above: The Test Industry's Failures." Accessible at www.nytimes.com/learning/general/specials/testing. A series on errors by testing companies with links to many related articles.

NOTES

1. Thomas J. Kane and Douglas O. Staiger, "Volatility in School Test Scores: Implications for Test-Based Accountability Systems," unpublished manuscript, Hoover Institution, Stanford University, Stanford, Calif., April 2001.

2. Jay P. Heubert and Robert M. Hauser, *Testing for Tracking, Promotion, and Grading* (Washington, D.C.: National Research Council, 1999), pp. 44-45.

3. Roughly half anyway. It depends on whether the college is using a "mean" or a "median" as its definition of average. Highly selective colleges are most likely to use a mean; open enrollment colleges are more likely to use a median. All of this is explained in more detail in later sections of this book.

4. Grant Wiggins, *Assessing Student Performance: Exploring the Purpose and Limits of Testing* (San Francisco: Jossey-Bass, 1993), p. 72.

5. F. Allan Hanson, *Testing, Testing: Social Consequences of the Examined Life* (Berkeley: University of California Press, 1993).

6. Alfie Kohn, *The Case Against Standardized Testing: Raising the Scores, Ruining the Schools* (Portsmouth, N.H.: Heinemann, 2000), p. 5.

7. Keppel was "commissioner" and not "secretary" because at the time the U.S. Department of Education was part of the U.S. Department of Health, Education, and Welfare and not a separate Cabinet-level department.

8. The five associations were the American Association of School Administrators, the National Association of Elementary School Principals, the National Association of Secondary School Principals, the National Education Association, and the American Educational Research Association.

9. Cited in Norman Fredericksen, Robert A. Mislevy, and Isaac A. Bejar, eds., *Test Theory for a New Generation of Tests* (Hillsdale, N.J.: Erlbaum, 1993).

10. National Research Council, *Knowing What Students Know: The Science and Design of Educational Assessment* (Washington, D.C.: National Academy Press, 2001), p. 26.

11. Ibid., pp. 292-94.

12. Some readers might have noticed that in some places on previous pages, I have referred to ranks as "scores." Technically, that is incorrect. A rank is a rank. Different scores are at different ranks, but the scores are not the ranks. Calling ranks scores is common in both writing and talking about tests because it is awkward to be absolutely correct. This confusion becomes important only when we forget that ranks alone actually obscure performance. International comparisons are often reported in ranks only. Tongues cluck over low-ranking countries. What this kind of reporting hides is that most of the countries' scores are very close. For instance, in one recent study of science in 41 nations, the United States ranked 19th, and *U.S. News & World Report* declared that this put us on a par with Bulgaria and Iceland. Bulgarian students did get only 4% more correct answers than American kids, but this vaulted them all the way to fifth place. Icelandic students got 6% fewer items correct than American students, and this dropped them all the way to 30th place.

13. Glaser invented the term, but almost the same concept was described by the father of educational testing, Edward L. Thorndike almost 50 years earlier.

14. Jason Millman, "Criterion-Referenced Testing 30 Years Later: Promise Broken, Promise Kept," *Educational Measurement, Issues and Practices*, Winter 1994, p. 19.

15. Lauren Resnick, *Education and Learning to Think* (Washington, D.C.: National Academy Press, 1987), p. 3.

16. Warwick P. Elley, *How in the World Do Students Read?* This book was originally published by the International Association for the Evaluation of Educational Achievement in The Hague; available in the U.S. through the International Reading Assocation, Newark, DE or at www.amazon.com.

17. Dave Barry, "The ABCs of the SATs," *Washington Post*, 12 October 1997.

18. Gerald W. Bracey, "SAT Scores: Miserable or Miraculous," *Education Week*, 21 November 1990.

19. Ralph Tyler, "Assessing the Progress of Education," *Phi Delta Kappan*, September 1965, pp. 13-16.

20. The evaluators hired by NAGB were Daniel Stufflebeam of Western Michigan University; Richard Jaeger of the University of North Carolina, Greensboro; and Michael Scriven of NOVA University.

21. Quoted in Stephen Jay Gould, *The Mismeasure of Man* (New York: Norton, 1981).